William Gaunt
was born in 1900 and was educated at
Hull Grammar School and at Worcester College, Oxford. His career included periods as Art Critic of the
Evening Standard, London, and as Special Correspondent
to *The Times* on art subjects. From the 1920s until his
death he was continually engaged in the editing of books
on art subjects and in art criticism, devoting himself
especially to the elucidation of English painting
in the nineteenth century.

WORLD OF ART

This famous series
provides the widest available
range of illustrated books on art in all its aspects.
If you would like to receive a complete list
of titles in print please write to:
THAMES AND HUDSON
30 Bloomsbury Street, London WC1B 3QP
In the United States please write to:
THAMES AND HUDSON INC.
500 Fifth Avenue, New York, New York 10110

D0109190

Printed in Singapore

William Gaunt

ENGLISH PAINTING
A Concise History

222 illustrations, 41 in color

Thames and Hudson

*Published in the United States of America in 1978 by
Thames and Hudson Inc., 500 Fifth Avenue,
New York, New York 10110
under the title* A Concise History of English Painting

© *Thames and Hudson Ltd, London 1964*
Reprinted 1993

Library of Congress Catalog Card Number 78-50968

Printed and bound in Singapore

Contents

Introduction

The general character of English painting is defined for us by the work of great individuals. In Hogarth its inclination towards the illustration of social life has a supreme example. In Gainsborough there is all of a native poetry of feeling. Devotion to landscape, ranging from a patriotic delight in the local scene to a romantic sense of far horizons, is summed up by Constable and Turner. An imaginative vein, warring at times with the observant description of natural fact, finds its exemplar in Blake. In none of these aspects can English painting be called 'classical'. Its excellence is of a different kind from that which belongs to the European tradition, the grandeur of Renaissance and Baroque art, the lucidity of aesthetic aim and reasoning which so distinguishes French painting. It takes on in the course of time the complexity and waywardness which are rather to be termed 'romantic'.

The complexity is in part due to the processes of social and economic change which so clearly separate one period from another; the age of the Tudors from the Middle Ages, the eighteenth from the seventeenth century, the nineteenth from the eighteenth, the modern age from that of Queen Victoria. English painting correspondingly proceeds in a fitful fashion. When the medieval tradition founders, it must slowly start again. It alternates between conservatism and individual ascents into freedom of expression. It changes in aspect with the variable relation of island and neighbouring continent.

After the 'Channel bridge' of the Middle Ages is broken under the Tudors European influence becomes 'foreign', though for a long stretch of time, and with some remarkable exceptions, painters from the Continent working in England predominate. They cannot be dissociated from the history of English art though it is a native evolution that results in the great creative outbursts of the eighteenth and early nineteenth centuries. Historically the affinities of English painting have been stronger with northern than with southern Europe, with the Netherlands in particular. A recurring tendency to isolationism has not perhaps been without some adverse effect in causing English painters to lag behind or exclude from view other and later developments of art on the European mainland. On the other hand their place apart from the European 'mainstream' has created a situation never lacking in interest. Independence of spirit has animated achievement as distinctive and original as that of Hogarth and Blake; at the same time a renewal of contact with vital developments elsewhere, such as is to be found in this century after a long separation in the Victorian Age, has given English painting a new impulse of creative energy. There has been in the past some tendency to be apologetic about or deprecate various aspects of its tradition, the 'literary' character of poetic or narrative products, the limiting demands of portraiture against which artists themselves have chafed, the prevalence of good taste as distinct from the expression of strong feeling, the want of 'plastic' virtues which has accompanied its linear bent, yet in each respect there are compensating values to be appreciated; and as Professor Ellis Waterhouse has remarked (*à propos* of English portraiture), 'Today it may seem more sensible to enjoy and value what our tradition has bequeathed us, rather than to repine over what it has not.' Surveyed as a whole, in present-day perspective, the history of English painting reveals an immense amount to be enjoyed and a number of outstanding individual contributions to art, the value of which is probably more evident now than at any previous time.

CHAPTER ONE

The Middle Ages and their legacy

It is usual to regard English painting as beginning with the Tudor period and for this there are several reasons. When Henry VIII abolished Papal authority in England in 1534 and ordered the dissolution of the monasteries in 1536 he automatically brought to an end the tradition of religious art as it had been practised in the Middle Ages and in monastic centres. The break was so complete that painting before and after seem entirely different things, in subject, style, and medium. Yet it is not only because the illuminated manuscript and devotional wall painting were replaced by secular portraiture that the subjects have been divorced. Medieval painting was not national in the modern sense, and often enough there is no telling whether it was the work of a native or foreign artist even when produced in England. A notable instance is the Wilton Diptych, showing Richard II presented to the Virgin and Child by two Patron Saints. The subject is English, the conception French. There remains the unverified or unverifiable possibility that it was painted by an Englishman trained in the French manner, though the evidence of style causes it to be ascribed in the National Gallery Catalogue to 'French School, *c*. 1395 (?)'.

1 Roundel of the Virgin and Child, *c*. 1260

Yet the fact remains that painting was practised in England for many hundreds of years before the first Tudor came to the throne, and that at various periods during that time certain technical attributes are to be found which reappear in more modern times and may be said to constitute a medieval legacy. The development of the linear design in which English artists have always excelled can be traced back to the earliest illuminations, which witness a first great flowering of Christian art in the British Isles. It may be called an Anglo-Hibernian art, brilliantly evolved in Irish monastic centres and brought to Northumbria in the seventh century. Containing some Byzantine elements its principal feature is that wonderful elaboration of interlaced ornament derived from the patterns of metalwork in the Celtic Iron Age, which is to be found in the Book of Kells and the Lindisfarne Gospel, its Northumbrian equivalent.

The linear style took its way southwards. It was practised in the *scriptoria* or monastic studios of York, St Albans, Glastonbury, Winchester, Canterbury. We now see something of that reciprocity of influence between England and the Continent of which there are later examples. The Celtic style had its effect on manuscript illumination in the Frankish Empire. In turn England in the Anglo-Saxon period was influenced by a style of free outline drawing, ultimately derived from classical models. The Carolingian Utrecht Psalter of the early ninth century, once kept at Canterbury Cathedral, with its freely sketched pen groups became a model for English artists, especially for those of Winchester, long a principal seat of

2 The Luttrel Psalter, *c.* 1340 Marginal illustration: Archery. An observant rendering of everyday aspects of life gives particular value to this East Anglian illuminated manuscript, executed for Sir Geoffrey Luttrell of Irnham Lincolnshire

Anglo-Saxon and later of Gothic art. The tinted outline in the tenth century already foreshadows the method of Rowlandson.

In the development of Gothic painting from the thirteenth century, England and France came close together, so close that it is possible to speak of an 'English Channel' School. Yet it is possible also to distinguish an English delicacy of line and a graceful elongation of the figure in which line plays an expressive part. Its quality is to be seen in the productions of the great school of St Albans where from 1236 until 1259 the English monk, Matthew Paris, took charge of the Abbey *scriptorium* (*Ill. 4*). Mainly known as a brilliant chronicler of the history of his time, a chronicle ending abruptly in 1259 when he died, he was also a talented artist, whose combination of delicate line with a certain tendency towards realism can be appreciated in his charming picture of himself at the feet of the Virgin and Child. His artistic administration at St Albans saw the production of a masterpiece in the roundel of the Virgin and Child, *c.* 1260 (*Ill. 1*), now in the Bishop's Chapel at Chichester, by an unknown but almost certainly English artist.

An English style, in which significance is concentrated on outline rather than the plastic or dimensional substance of the figure, is characteristic in the psalters of the thirteenth and fourteenth centuries. The feeling behind it was eventually to be given expression at the beginning of the nineteenth century by William Blake in his insistence on the 'determinate' line and the repugnance with which he viewed the material contours rounded by the light and shade of Correggio. It is not unreasonable to see in Blake a continuance of an instinctive tendency implanted long before. The feeling for line, together with great refinements of colour, beautifully appears in English medieval embroidery, especially that of the thirteenth and fourteenth centuries, famous throughout Europe as 'opus Anglicanum', in its pictorial aspect reflecting the work of painters who supplied the embroidery workshops with designs (*Ill. 3*).

The products of the Gothic Age in England as they have come down to us are most impressive on a small scale and perhaps in this we may see a tendency which has continued in English painting. There is no such tradition of monumental scale as steadily developed elsewhere. Time in any case has dealt harshly with wall painting, reduced to fragments by decay or mischance or deliberately defaced and covered over by Puritanical zeal. Copies and fragments give but little idea of the scheme of decoration of St Stephen's Chapel, Westminster, carried out under the supervision of Master Hugh of St Albans between 1327 and 1370 and ruthlessly destroyed by the architect James Wyatt in the early nineteenth century for alterations

3, 4 An example of 'opus Anglicanum' embroidery (*left*) showing the mature character of design in this 'English Work'. The *Virgin and Child*, by Matthew Paris (*right*), is an early and exquisite example of a line drawing heightened with tints of colour

to the fabric. There is only a hint of its heraldic splendour in the despairing eulogies of Wyatt's time – the antiquary John Carter's praise of its sublimity, John Topham's testimony to its 'universal blaze of colour and magnificence'. A Late Gothic example of note is the series of wall paintings in Eton College Chapel, the *Miracles of the Virgin* (*Ill. 6*), painted between 1479 and 1488 by an artist called William Baker of whom nothing seems to be known. Whitewashed over during the Reformation period, they remained unknown until 1847 and were not completely uncovered until 1923. The paintings are of interest as showing a new link between England and the Netherlands, and indeed the artist may have been Flemish. Something of the lively handling of the manuscript painter appears in the decorations, simple and often quite summary, of local churches, and in such developments of panel painting as the retable of Norwich Cathedral (*Ill. 5*), the work possibly of a member or members of a Norwich family called Ocle.

Faculties which could remain untouched by the collapse of tradition after the disastrous fifteenth century and the advent of a new age, apart from considerations of style, were an observation and a delight in recording scenes and incidents of everyday life which are often encountered in later centuries. Already the Bayeux Tapestry of *c.* 1080, probably executed in England and closely related in its graphic vigour to Anglo-Saxon

5 The retable in Norwich Cathedral provides an example of fourteenth-century East Anglian painting. Each of the five panels has its distinct and expressive design, in which line is a dominant factor; at the same time they come together in harmonious unity

models, shows the narrative zest and the keen eye for detail which, in different guise, Hogarth was later to employ. The building of ships, the authentic incident of embarkation and disembarkation, the preparation and nature of a banquet, the accurate delineation of armour, all mount up to a picture of society as well as an account of conquest.

The remarkable series of psalters of the thirteenth to fourteenth centuries mainly produced in East Anglia introduces, quite irrelevantly to its devotional purposes, scenes of agricultural work, sports and pastimes, and the animal grotesques to which the word 'babwyneries' was applied. The Gorleston Psalter of *c.* 1300, the Ormesby Psalter, Queen Mary's Psalter, the Luttrell Psalter (*Ill. 2*), give fascinating pictures of ploughing, sowing, reaping, wrestlers, players on musical instruments, bear-baiting, and animals fancifully portrayed in human dress and occupation. Here may be found at its source the English aptitude for genre.

Yet to all outward appearance English painting starts again after the Wars of the Roses. The fifteenth century was one of medieval decline. English painting came to a halt at a time when painting in Italy was invested with the full splendour of the Renaissance.

6 Eton College Chapel contains a unique surviving example of painting on a large scale in fifteenth-century England in the *Miracles of the Virgin* by William Baker. It shows in style the influence of the Netherlands, closely related to England at the time for reasons of trade, but an English character may be discerned in a graceful linear element

CHAPTER TWO

Painting in the Tudor and Jacobean periods

When the monasteries were dissolved, religious painting as an annex of Catholicism inevitably disappeared and the possibility of any such new development as that launched in Europe in the sixteenth century by the Counter-Reformation was obviously precluded, indeed would have been a treasonable activity. The local centres of culture having vanished, the tendency of painting to be centralized in London and in the service of the court was affirmed. Secular patronage now insisted on portraiture, and the habit grew up of using foreign painters – an artificial replacement of the old, international interchange of artists and craftsmen.

Portraiture had existed in the Middle Ages, especially in the form of royal iconography. An example is the portrait of Richard II in Westminster Abbey by an unknown artist, still impressive in design though it has been much repainted. Yet the sixteenth century, it has to be remembered, was the age of Humanism which had created a new interest in the individual personality that the medieval icon did not satisfy. Foreign painters were evidently favoured as having been trained in a more realistic school than the English, and thus being more capable of producing a satisfactory likeness. At one time a *Lady Margaret Beaufort* formerly in the National Portrait Gallery was cited as an example of accomplished pre-Tudor mastery, but this has been shown to be a later overpainting and no longer appears in the Collection. Another anonymous painting of this lady, shows a more characteristic rigidity (*Ill. 7*).

It does not appear that English patrons were as yet connoisseurs to any appreciable extent. They had none of that delight in beauty which caused the Renaissance princes of Italy to commission illustrations of classical legend. They required simply an accurate likeness and the ability to do detailed justice to their finery of dress and its accessories. Henry VIII, who was no Francis I, anxious to heighten his prestige by a brilliant art circle, wanted no more than this. The portrait of Henry by Hans Holbein the Younger (*Ill. 8*) in the version of the Thyssen-Bornemisza Collection (regarded as the only surviving authentic representation of the King from Holbein's own hand) records all the desired facts though it adds the stamp of character which only a great artist could give.

It was not by Henry VIII's express wish that the German master came to England. He arrived at the age of twenty-nine with a recommendation to Sir Thomas More from Erasmus and the hope of finding more profitable employment than in Basle, then beset by religious dissension. Like Van Dyck in the century following he is inseparable from an account of English painting though his work is to be viewed in a much wider context. Born in Augsburg in 1497, trained by his father and Hans Burgkmair, acquainted with the art both of Italy and France, he had a broad artistic culture and a superb range of ability, apt not only for portraiture but for religious composition, mural painting and the arts of design. He spent in all some thirteen years in England, first from 1526 to 1528, staying with More at Beaufort House in Chelsea, when he painted the portrait (1527) now in the Frick Collection, New York, and worked on the group of Sir Thomas and his family, the impressive conception of which can be appreciated from a surviving drawing at Basle. He returned in 1532, became official court painter to Henry VIII in 1536 and died in London in 1543.

In considering his place in English art, two questions arise: what effect England had on him and what effect he had on

7 *Lady Margaret Beaufort* (*Countess of Richmond*), an example of rigidly stylized portraiture by an unknown artist of the late fifteenth century, the subject being the mother of Henry VII

8 *Portrait of Henry VIII*, by Hans Holbein, generally accepted as the only surviving portrait of the King from the artist's own hands. It sets the key of Tudor portraiture in the precise delineation of feature and the elaborate treatment of accessories

English painting. His power to bring a living person authentically before us never failed, though a difference can be observed between the massive treatment of dimension in the More portrait and his later tendency towards a flat background and linear pattern. This may indicate some deference to his patrons' more elementary tastes but never lacks a beautiful simplicity and refinement, as in the portrait of Anne of Cleves and that masterpiece of 1538, the portrait of Christina of Denmark, Duchess of Milan, for which he had only a three hours' sitting. His sense of character in itself gives an English appearance to his work, as can be appreciated from the wonderful drawings of members of the court at Windsor. One can differentiate the character of his paintings of the German merchants of the London Steelyard, for example the *Georg Gisze*.

What survives of the larger portrait groups, apart from *The Ambassadors*, 1533, which seems a kind of demonstration of skill in the painting of detail, shows a more documentary convention, as may be seen in the much damaged painting for the Barber-Surgeons which belongs to his last years. It suggests a certain repression of Holbein's abilities on a large scale. His influence on English painting was exerted through the individual portrait. That it was considerable cannot be questioned, though there is little of direct succession. Assistants no doubt were employed on the numerous variants of the royal portrait which still exist, but they remain in obscurity.

A good many question-marks attach to the portrait of a man in a black cap (*Ill. 9*), dated 1545, and inscribed 'faict par Jehan Bettes Anglois': why, for instance, the inscription should have been in French; where the picture was painted; who was the sitter and, indeed, who was John Bettes. What is clear is that the portrait is an excellent work in the style of Holbein and may well have been the product of someone who worked in his studio. The influence of Holbein, however, is specific in the art of miniature painting, which he practised in his later years, and such examples as *Mrs Pemberton* (*Ill. 10*) and

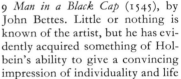

9 *Man in a Black Cap* (1545), by John Bettes. Little or nothing is known of the artist, but he has evidently acquired something of Holbein's ability to give a convincing impression of individuality and life

Katharine Howard, were to inspire the exquisite art of Nicholas Hilliard, which shines with a native lustre in the Elizabethan Age.

Before considering Hilliard, it is needful to pause before the spectacle of various foreign painters, visiting or settling in the England of the Tudors and in the 'Jacobethan' period of Elizabeth I and James I. Most of them came from the Netherlands and were competent craftsmen of a secondary order, often reflecting in some degree the Mannerist style prevailing in the sixteenth century. There is the Netherlandish painter Guillim Scrots (variously spelt Scroets or Stretes), active in the mid sixteenth century and a court painter to Henry VIII and Edward VI, who specialized in the full-length portrait; the German, Gerlach Flicke, who worked in London from 1547 until his death in 1558 and adopted something of Holbein's manner; most notably Hans Eworth, a Flemish painter born and trained in Antwerp, who was active in England for at least a quarter of a century, from *c.* 1550 until 1574. Eworth

10 *Portrait of Mrs Pemberton* (1540–3), by Hans Holbein, whose influence was most fruitful in the miniature portraits produced during his residence in England, with their concentration of jewel-like colour and delicacy of modelling

can be viewed as a Mannerist in the striking early portrait (1550) of Sir John Luttrell with its allegorical references to the sitter's maritime and martial adventures. He later reverted to the allegory with flattering intent in his *Queen Elizabeth and the three Goddesses*, of 1569 (*Ill. 11*). A second phase of his painting was Holbeinesque; a third, the development of the heavily stylized costume piece which became typically Elizabethan. He may have owed something to that international figure of portraiture, Anthonis Mor, who came to England for a period in the reign of Queen Mary, but he had a strong individuality of his own.

What of native English talent? George Gower (active 1575, d. 1596), who became Serjeant Painter to Queen Elizabeth in 1581, was an artist whose work has a considerable charm and a feeling for line which is seen to advantage in his portraits of Sir Thomas and Lady Kytson (*Ill. 12*). There are anonymous sixteenth-century portraits in the Tate Gallery which have a simplicity or lightness of touch that seems to distinguish them

11 *Queen Elizabeth and the three Goddesses* (1569), by Hans Eworth. Allegorical or symbolic composition in the Elizabethan Age was still linked with portraiture. A revised version of the Judgement of Paris, this painting shows the Queen with an orb instead of an apple, self-awarded to the confusion of Juno, who has lost a shoe, an armed Minerva and Venus with Cupid. Windsor Castle is in the background

12 George Gower was a delightful if not a great painter and the portraits of Sir Thomas and Lady Kytson (1573), well illustrate an English inheritance in their feeling for linear effect. They display in addition a refined decorative sense and if the artist does not bring out character with Holbein's peculiar power, he is not lacking in perception of individuality in facial traits

from the weightier products of foreign origin and also from the astonishing development of almost Byzantine formality, the series of anonymous 'cult portraits' of the Queen, devised as abstract symbols of majesty and with a tremendous lavishness of detail, of which the 'Ditchley' Portrait, *c.* 1593 (*Ill. 13*), is an example.

In contrast, and to an Englishman the most emotionally appealing product of the Elizabethan Age, is the art of the miniature. In its intimate nature it was at the opposite pole from the formalized images which represented autocratic government and from the factory products of such foreign groups as the related De Critz and Gheeraerts families whose output has given rise to many dubious attributions. The miniature was an art with an entirely different technique and origin from that of the foreign oil painters, a development from the manuscript illumination, the title 'limner' being itself a corruption of 'illuminator'. Painters in the Netherlands seem to have been the first to substitute the small-scale portrait for the religious miniature and some were employed at the court of Henry VIII, for example the 'paintrix', Lavinia Teerlinck, of whose work nothing remains, and Luke Horenbout who is said to have given some lessons in the art to Holbein. Gem-like conception, clear and brilliant colour, a reduction of modelling to decorative simplicity were qualities which Holbein displays in his own magnificent fashion. They were studied by Hilliard, who says of Holbein that his 'manner of limning I have ever imitated'. Hilliard, however, is distinct in the fresh and intimate character of his work, and the poetic feeling which makes him the kin of the Elizabethan lyricists. His miniatures were small jewels – it is significant that he was the son of a goldsmith and was able to set his miniatures in a jewelled framework with entire unity of effect (*Ill. 14*). Such works were studied by the noble patron as delightful objects in themselves, and as intimate revelations of character and sentiment of an opposite kind from the formal attitude presented to the world in the large panel. His self-portrait at the age of thirty reveals with what alertness he observed fleeting

13 The 'Ditchley' Portrait of Elizabeth I, of *c.* 1593, by an unknown artist. An extraordinary development of Elizabethan portraiture is represented by later paintings of the Queen which become formalized symbols of majesty. An almost Byzantine result can be appreciated in this deliberately stylized portrait in which the Queen stands dominant on the map of England

14, 15 The art of Nicholas Hilliard is exemplified here in intimate portraiture and poetic feeling. The miniature (*left*) is a *Portrait of Drake* (so-called), of 1581. In the famous *Portrait of an Unknown Man* (*right*) the flames of love, so much a property of amorous verse, become a pictorial metaphor, and a background against which his dark hair and finely embroidered grey shirt gain exquisite and unusual value of colour

16, 17 Hilliard's *Youth leaning against a Tree among Roses*, of *c.* 1588 (*opposite left*), provides a beautiful equivalent to the Elizabethan sonnet. Style and content are in entire harmony and the work is full of inspired passages: the varied tracery of rose-blossom against the black cloak, the dapple of leaves on the youth's white hose. There is a difference analogous to that of poetry and prose between this and the *Young Man leaning against a Tree*, of *c.* 1590 (*opposite right*) by Isaac Oliver, though Oliver's 'prose' is also a finely fashioned instrument

expression. His *George Clifford, Earl of Cumberland* shows the verve he could give to line and gesture, while the famous portrait of a *Youth leaning against a Tree among Roses* (*Ill.* 16), suffering the pangs of love as a Latin motto indicates, is the masterpiece of Elizabethan pictorial art. The equivalent of an Elizabethan sonnet is that equally well-known miniature of an unknown man (*Ill.* 15), the flames of whose passion become a metaphorical background.

Hilliard had a brilliant pupil in Isaac Oliver, offspring of a French Huguenot family, born in Rouen and brought as a child to London by his refugee parents. There is a superficial likeness in their work, for example in the frequent use of a

26

brilliant blue background, though there are differences of more importance. Oliver's affinities were with the art of the Continent. By marriage he became connected with the Flemish painter-coterie in London and the full-size portrait of the Flemish artists was really his ideal. To say that he was more of a representational painter than Hilliard is to say that he lacked the poetic spirit and decorative charm of the latter, substituting, even on a small scale, more of realism and more of formal splendour.

The realism appears in the unfinished miniature of the Queen (with the signs of age which no doubt she thought all too evident) and in the portrait of a young aristocrat which has been identified as that of Sir Philip Sidney (*Ill. 17*). If it is compared with Hilliard's lover among the roses, the difference of style and outlook between the two artists strikingly appears. Oliver's desire to give a full-dress magnificence to the miniature appears in such elaborate works as the *Sir Anthony Mildmay* of 1605, and the *Richard Sackville, Earl of Dorset* of 1616 (*Ill. 18*), in which the panoply of arms and the rich appurtenances of an interior setting play their part. In such works one can see the beginning of the process by which the miniature lost its independence as an art form and became a subsidiary of the oil painting, either in imitation of its technique or as a direct copy. A transitional phase is represented by the two miniaturists' sons, Lawrence Hilliard and Peter Oliver, who continued in the family vocation. Their work is not without attraction, as examples in the Victoria and Albert Museum's Collection show, though in the painting of Peter Oliver especially one can see the reaction from bright colour and the development of the chiaroscuro which it had been a main tenet of Nicholas Hilliard's art to avoid.

18 While making use of the miniature painter's special prerogative of glowing colour for its own sake, as seen in the blue of the curtains and details of dress and pattern, the character of this *Portrait of Richard Sackville, Earl of Dorset* (1616) by Isaac Oliver is that of the large-scale oil painting, as practised by Marcus Gheeraerts the Younger, Oliver's brother-in-law, the full-length figure being dimensionally represented in the perspective of an interior. Hilliard adopted this mode of design in his later work, but Oliver more clearly shows the trend towards realistic presentation

CHAPTER THREE

The Stuart period

In painting the Stuart period has several phases, though the import of foreign portrait painters remained a constant factor. The reign of James I (1603–25) was to some extent a continuance of the Elizabethan Age. Hilliard and Oliver were active for many years after the death of the Queen in 1603. A remarkable individual appears in the person of Sir Nathaniel Bacon, (*c.* 1585–1627), step-nephew of the great Francis Bacon, unusual as a gentleman amateur who condescended to practise what was then generally looked on as the craft of the artisan. The existing works by him show an accomplishment in which there is nothing of the amateur in the modern sense of the word but rather a professional mastery. Free of the restrictions imposed on the portrait painters, he embarks on such an elaborate composition of figure and still-life as *The Cookmaid* (*Ill. 19*) and carries it off with great verve, in a manner which shows an unusual and intelligent appreciation of the aims of the Italianate Utrecht school in which the naturalism of Caravaggio can ultimately be divined. Considered in a wide context he has, perhaps, been overrated by some modern writers on art, though in a local and contemporaneous relation he shines out the more in contrast with the unventuresome mediocrity of the workman-portraitist.

Sir Nathaniel gives evidence of a new trend in taste in which the younger generation of the Jacobean time, its 'virtuosi', reacted against the elementary and Philistine criteria of their elders. Italy, so long outside the insular ken, again came into

19 Sir Nathaniel Bacon's *The Cookmaid* is a surprising exception in English painting of the early seventeenth century. The ably executed composition shows how a virtuoso amateur could escape professional restrictions and assimilate an 'advanced' European style

view through the architectural learning and genius of Inigo Jones. Henry Frederick, Prince of Wales, eldest son of James I, and the young Prince Charles, later Charles I, gained a broader view of art through Jones and through Thomas Howard, Earl of Arundel, who formed the first great art collection in England. In portraiture at first there is a moderate improvement, if we are so to describe the departure from Elizabethan formality in the work of the imported Dutch painters with whom Stuart portraiture begins. Paul van Somer (1576–1621) born in Antwerp but trained in Holland, who came to England in 1616, was the earliest of these Netherlanders. His portrait of Anne of Denmark with groom, horse, and hounds in front of the Palace of Oatlands (with Inigo Jones's new gateway) (*Ill. 20*)

20 The growing realism of painting, Dutch in inspiration, in the early seventeenth century has an early instance in *Portrait of Queen Anne of Denmark* (1617) by Paul van Somer, somewhat stilted in manner but an elaborate effort to add to likeness details of place and rural diversion

makes a step towards realism, though still stiff and cramped in composition. Daniel Mytens is a more considerable artist. Mytens (*c.* 1590–1642), born and trained at The Hague, came to England before 1618, working at first for Arundel and being fully occupied with royal portraiture after Charles I's accession until his eventual return to Holland. A master of the full-length he was able to convey character and to pose his sitters in a natural manner, while he also showed a distinguished colour sense. His *Charles I as Prince of Wales* (*Ill. 21*), the *Duke of Hamilton as a Boy*, and the *Robert, 2nd Earl of Warwick* give their evidence of these qualities.

Cornelius Johnson, born in London in 1593, came of one of those families which had fled to England during the religious troubles of the Netherlands. He worked for James I and Charles I and was a painter whom a certain charm of style seems to place in Hilliard's succession and in some relation with Marcus Gheeraerts the Younger (1561–1635), whose pupil he may have been. Working in England until the Civil War period – he departed for Holland in 1643 – he showed an advance towards the elegance of which a greater example now appeared in the person of Van Dyck.

Charles I retained in his employment the painters who had served his father, but the great change of attitude to living artists which was the result of his enlightened connoisseurship and appreciation of the masterpieces for which his agents scoured Europe soon became evident. He sought to attract to his court not merely competent workmen but men of genius. Though he could not hope to win away Rubens from the service of the Regent of the Netherlands, the Infanta Isabella, he could load the Baroque master with insular honours and obtain from his hand the great ceiling of the Inigo Jones Banqueting Hall. That he induced Van Dyck to settle in England in 1632 was of the greatest significance for English painting.

Then aged thirty-three, Van Dyck was at the height of his ability. He had profited by seven years spent in Italy during

21 More elegant in style than Van Somer, Daniel Mytens has a place of distinction in Stuart portraiture and his paintings of Charles I are individual in character, though overshadowed by the achievement of his great younger contemporary, Van Dyck

which time he studied the great Venetians and especially Titian. He had acquired all the resource of Baroque art in arrangement and variety of pose and gesture. He was ideally suited to express the spirit of an autocratic régime – the essence of Baroque painting. Courtly grace and ease, combined with a certain dignified aloofness, decorative splendour, learned devices of composition translated from Baroque religious painting into terms of the portrait group, were displayed in his art in a way which made his predecessors in England look rather wooden in comparison. The relation of figure and background – landscape or stately glimpse of architecture – the aristocratic ease of stance, the expressive pose of hands, the complementary character of two or more figures which he established, remained characteristic of English portraiture for more than a century.

Working in England (with some absences abroad) for eleven years until his death in 1641, married to an English woman, Mary, daughter of Sir Patrick Ruthven, living in state at a house at Blackfriars, knighted and honoured by the King, Van Dyck has an English existence in which he seems far removed from the Flemish master who painted opulent religious compositions at Antwerp. He gives the impression of reacting sensitively to his environment, of taking on something of the poetic attitude which existed subtly in the English atmosphere. His portraits of Charles, refined and melancholy, reflect it; it pervades the silvery tones of his portrait of Henrietta Maria (*Ill. 22*); it appears unexpectedly in the landscape sketches preserved in the British Museum, which give the feeling of English country in a way not to be found again until Constable's time. In portraiture he has an heir in the eighteenth century as magnificently in sympathy with his genius as Thomas Gainsborough.

22 Van Dyck was the source of inspiration to English portraiture, both in groups and single portraits. His *Portrait of Henrietta Maria* of *c.* 1639 is a classic example of the grace and refinement of detail and colour which find many reflections in the later part of the seventeenth century

Yet in the refinement of Van Dyck there were the seeds of an artificiality which became more pronounced as the seventeenth century went on. Though he cannot be said to have lacked a sense of character, of the essential humanity which is to be found for instance in his portrait of Thomas Killigrew and Thomas Carew (Royal Collection), character was to some extent veiled and modified by the artificial nature of the exclusive society which he served, of ideas of government and authority which were already being roughly contested when he died. The approach of the Civil War stripped away the polish and brought out a sterner strain of character no less in the aristocratic supporters of the royalist cause than in their democratic opponents. In the realism with which he depicted the militant Cavalier, William Dobson (1610–46) marks a breakaway from Van Dyckian elegance. With the assertion of a sturdy simplicity of approach in which he was decidedly original he could be termed by Aubrey 'the most excellent painter that England hath yet bred'.

There is little enough indication of how Dobson was trained. Born in London, the son of a government official, he seems to have had some part in the decoration of Francis Bacon's house, Gorhambury. A tradition, repeated by Horace Walpole, places him for a time with Sir Robert Peake, picture dealer and printseller, 'with whom he had the advantage of copying some pictures by Titian and Tintoret'. There is reason to think he was the pupil of the German decorative painter Francis Cleyn who came to England from Denmark, where he was employed by Christian IV, and worked under the patronage of James I and Charles I. Mr Oliver Millar, whose enthusiasm and research have done so much to assign Dobson his proper place, suggests that through Cleyn he was able to study the Venetian paintings in the great royal collection, Venetian influence being evident in his colour and style, though with no trace of Van Dyck's own learned borrowings from the same source. Dobson comes suddenly into prominence in royalist Oxford after the Civil War had broken out.

He stayed there, painting members of the royal family and royalist officers in the stormy years from 1642 to 1646, leaving the city in April of the latter year, two months before it fell to the Parliamentary forces. He died in poverty in St Martin's Lane in the following October.

The painting of Endymion Porter, the friend and agent of Charles I in the purchase of works of art, is generally accounted Dobson's masterpiece. The decorative sculptural details of the composition may suggest the subject's connoisseurship, but the most striking aspect of the work is its realism. Though Endymion Porter is portrayed as a sportsman who has just shot a hare, there is a stern look about his features which seems to convey that this is wartime. The elegance of Van Dyck would have been out of accord with the spirit of beleaguered royalist Oxford. In happier times, the officers he paints would have been gay, perhaps foppish and languidly affected; now, as Dobson conveys, they are virile, resolute, tense, as in his brooding *Prince Rupert*, the splendid *Portrait of an Unknown Man* (*Ill. 24*), and the *John, 1st Baron Byron* (*Ill. 23*). The soldierly pose of the latter contrasts with the ornate columns behind him, an accessory of the kind which recalls the ornamental detail of the Mortlake tapestries on which Dobson had worked. In these portraits he shows a truthful feeling for character, an absence of artificiality which does not otherwise appear strongly until the following century.

The solemnity of the times is also reflected in the portraiture produced during the Commonwealth period and one would naturally expect an even greater rejection of elegance than that of Dobson during the Puritan dominance. Indeed a prospect of unsparing realism is set out in Cromwell's grimly jocular admonition to 'Mr Lilly' – the Sir Peter Lely of the Restoration – to 'remark all these ruffness, pimples, warts' and paint 'everything as you see me'. The corresponding painter to Dobson on the Parliamentary side, however, Robert Walker (*c.* 1605/ 10–56/8), was a much less original artist and still closely imitated Van Dyck's graceful style. While he could paint the

23 This detail of the three-quarter-length portrait of a royalist officer in *c*. 1644, *John, 1st Baron Byron*, brings out the breadth and vigour of William Dobson's art in which there is an individuality owing little to Van Dyck

24 Dobson's *Portrait of an Unknown Man* of *c*. 1643 shows an independence new in English painting in its unconventional alertness of characterization and brilliant contrasts of colour. The sculptured figure apparently representing Geography and the ship in the background suggest that the sitter was a naval officer

features of Cromwell (*Ill. 25*) or Hampden with some appreciation of their Puritan character he could, quite incongruously, place the head of Cromwell on body and armour taken from Van Dyck's portrait of Sir Edmund Verney. It was indeed a common and artistically reprehensible practice of the time to regard figure and gesture as so much stock property to be used again and again with only a change of head.

On the whole in the disturbed seventeenth century artists were looked on as beings apart from political and ideological conflict. They painted the principal figures of the successive and conflicting régimes without apparently either feeling or being accused of disloyalty, though at the same time their style was liable to be affected by variations in political and social climate. A striking instance is given by Sir Peter Lely (1618–80) who is usually associated exclusively with the frivolous court of Charles II. Originally Peter van der Faes, he came to England first in 1641, a Dutch painter trained at Haarlem, to paint the marriage portrait of William of Orange and Charles I's daughter Mary. Settling in England and adopting the name Lely from that of a family property at The Hague, as still a young man he shows the great influence Van Dyck had on him. He painted with success during the Commonwealth though a certain reversion appeared in his work to his native Dutch realism and can be seen in the forceful portrait of Cromwell. The richness of the Dutch tradition can be appreciated in the group portrait of himself and family (*Ill. 26*), a *tour de force* in which he seems to enjoy a 'painter's holiday' free of the restrictions imposed by a patron. A notable series of portraits painted for Sir Ralph Bankes's house at Kingston Lacy, including that of Lady Jenkinson, Bankes's daughter, in *c.* 1660–62, shows his pre-Restoration style in admirable dignity. Mannerisms and affectations grew on him as the favoured painter of Charles II and the chosen portrayer of the beauties of his court. To do Lely justice it must be admitted that there is a certain correspondence between style and subject which could not otherwise have been attained.

25 While Dobson applied a new directness to portrayal of the Royalist Party, Robert Walker,
his equivalent on the Roundhead side, and a less original artist, still used the aristocratic conventions of Van Dyck, somewhat incongruously as in this *Portrait of Cromwell*

26 Lely was an artist of flexible gifts as this spirited example of the conversation piece, *The Artist and his Family* of *c.* 1658, shows. He is so much associated with the portrayal of court beauties in the reign of Charles II that the departure from a standardized product is striking, though the painting contains much that is characteristic. The self-portrait with a touch of humour recalls an ability in male portraiture more evident in the Commonwealth period than in his Restoration phase. The small children are delightfully brought to life, though his debt to Van Dyck is plain to see in the figures to the right

Nevertheless, the work of his busy 'picture factory' in Covent Garden evidently tended to become both monotonous and superficial. There is some point in the criticism attributed to Robert Walker that his 'Pictures was all Brothers and sisters'.

The miniaturist Samuel Cooper is another artist whose work spans the century and in spite of its small scale he stands out, as Hilliard did earlier, as the most exquisite artist of the age. With him the miniature arrived at that point to which it had been gradually tending, of portraiture scarcely distinguishable in style, light and shade, and strength of effect, from oil painting except by its size. Size indeed was not regarded as an important factor by his admiring contemporaries who would pay almost as much for one of his miniatures as for a large

picture by Lely. Born in 1609, Cooper was a pupil of his
uncle John Hoskins, also an artist of considerable ability, who
worked for Charles I and was much employed by the King
and others in making miniature copies after Van Dyck. The
influence of Van Dyck was passed on to Hoskins's pupil-
assistant. Cooper was able, however, to apply a delicate sense
of detail and a strong feeling for character in a thoroughly
original way. Flourishing before, during, and after civil strife
he gave as remarkable and extensive a record of his time as
any. He has left brilliant portraits alike of Cromwell and
Charles II, concentrating dramatically on the features as in
the unfinished sketch on vellum of Oliver Cromwell in the
collection of the Duke of Buccleuch. He painted charming

43

27 The miniatures of Samuel Cooper, such as this one of the *Duchess of Cleveland*, have no trace of the jewel-like quality so notable in Hilliard, but are exquisite products of the Restoration period

portraits of women without making use of a flattering convention. In his own time his reputation was international, and he remains on a special pinnacle. There were many other Stuart miniaturists, excellent in their way – Cooper's brother Alexander, Nicholas Dixon, David des Granges, Richard Gibson, the Beale family, Thomas Flatman – but Samuel Cooper, as a subtle and original artist, stands alone (*Ill. 27*).

Viewed generally, the age of Charles II together with the brief pendant of his brother's reign and that of William and Mary (which was only a 'revolution', monarchically speaking) is more notable for the developments of science and architecture than of pictorial art. Sir Christopher Wren is its representative figure and in comparison with his grandeur Lely's ability to portray court favourites in languishing attitudes dwindles in value. Even so, leaving Cooper out of account and as far as portrait painting is concerned, Lely had no rival. A number of other portrait painters claim the attention of the historian and are of interest by reason of their subjects without being greatly moving from an aesthetic standpoint. Among Lely's own pupils Willem Wissing (1656–87), the Dutch-born painter, was a follower of some competence who does not come up to his master. John Greenhill (*c.* 1644–76) is of some

28 The formal aspect of Caro-
lean portraiture is ably represented by John Michael Wright,
rather than Lely, as in this
painting of life-size which depicts *Charles II Enthroned* in *c*.
1661 under a canopy of State in
the revived splendour of coro-
nation robes, and with the
crown, orb, and sceptre specially
made for the occasion

29 Wright's *Portrait of Sir Neil O'Neill*
of Killylagh, an Irish Jacobite who
fought for James II in Scotland, less
formal in treatment than the portrait of
Charles II, is equally elaborate in its
representation of the national dress of
an Irish chieftain and his attendant.
Though Wright was not a great artist,
he here achieves a dramatic effect which
made this one of his most highly
esteemed works (*c*. 1679)

little note as one of the first artists to depict English actors in costume. John Michael Wright (1617–?1700) achieves formal magnificence in his *Charles II Enthroned* (*Ill. 28*) and combines an attractive bravura with an apparently accurate representation of the costume of an Irish chieftain in his portrait of the Irish Jacobite Sir Neil O'Neill (*Ill. 29*). John Riley (1646–91), pupil of the Dutch-born painter Gerard Soest, was an artist whose work is distinguished by a grave reticence. In succession to Lely he painted many eminent people, including Dryden, and some minor folk, as for example the aged housemaid Bridget Holmes (*Ill. 30*), though he was never free from a certain stiffness and a dullness which came from the employment of uninspired assistants.

Two factors break the uniformity of the later seventeenth century; first, the emergence of other forms of painting than the portraiture which seemed to dominate all artistic life in England; and second, certain changes in portrait painting, exemplified by Sir Godfrey Kneller, which bring it a stage nearer to the great eighteenth century. The lack of variety in English art is the more striking when one considers, on the one hand the number of genres which flourished in Holland and the southern Netherlands, the scenes of popular life, the landscapes, the paintings of animals and birds, the still-life and flower pieces; and, on the other, the magnificence of Baroque and decorative painting in the France of Louis XIV and his powerful impresario of the arts, Charles Le Brun. A faint reflection of each, however, now began to appear in England. Yet, as in portraiture, minor foreign artists were mainly employed to satisfy the awakening desire for some pictorial rendering of place and scene and for some decorative interior adornment of the great houses now being built in a more or less Baroque style.

The foreign artists who introduced new genres of painting seem to have been precursors with something of a delayed influence, rather than to have had an immediate English following. Thus the Van de Veldes, father and son, who came

30 Described by Horace Walpole as 'one of the best native painters who have flourished in England', John Riley seems to have been overshadowed by Lely and Kneller, though unlike them he was not confined to portraying the upper strata of society. In this *Portrait of Bridget Holmes* of 1686 he shows an attractive quality of observation and unassuming style

to England in 1672 to paint for Charles II, introduced a specialized technique of painting ships, sea, and marine warfare which found its continuance after their time in the work of Charles Brooking, Samuel Scott, and Peter Monamy. The long-term influence is especially striking in Turner's study of Willem van de Velde the Younger, a hundred years after the latter's death.

The Flemish artist Jan Siberechts and the Czech artist Wenceslaus Hollar (especially in watercolour drawings) anticipate the eighteenth-century 'discovery' of England in landscape and topography. It is strange to think that in a country later so renowned for landscape it was previously virtually unknown. As a painter of battle and hunting scenes in which the mounted horseman was prominent Jan Wyck (1652–1700) may be looked on as the precursor of the later line of sporting artists which begins with John Wootton. One English painter of animals, birds, and the chase deserves notice, Francis Barlow (?1626–1702), whose paintings and drawings are both firmly and conventionally outlined after the fashion of Hollar. It was a style which made the paintings suitable as decorative panels in an interior, though the drawings, of which there are good examples in the British Museum and Courtauld Institute of Art, London, are the most spirited of his works.

The revived Catholic tendencies of the Stuarts also inclined favour towards the European Baroque in the form of decorative mural painting. The infiltration of this style did not necessarily have a religious connotation, but its fitness to regal and aristocratic purpose commended it. Antonio Verrio and Louis Laguerre, Italian and French respectively but both experienced in the version of the Baroque which prevailed in the France of Louis XIV, applied a new grandiosity to the walls and ceilings of royal and noble dwellings. The famous line of Pope 'where sprawl the saints of Verrio and Laguerre' has perpetuated a certain contempt for their efforts in which there was always a sediment of Puritan and democratic bias.

48

They were indeed expert decorators rather than great artists, Laguerre the better artist of the two. The work of Verrio at Windsor Castle and Hampton Court and of Laguerre at Chatsworth and Blenheim especially, combines largeness of painted space with architecture in an effect of magnificence.

The arrival of Venetian decorative painters in the early years of the eighteenth century, Giovanni Antonio Pellegrini and Sebastiano and Marco Ricci, brought in a fresh phase of mural painting in which appear the lighter graces of the Rococo art which Tiepolo was to develop to its full extent in Venice. They worked for English noblemen of cultivated taste, the Duke of Manchester, the Earl of Burlington, and others. The allegorical paintings by Sebastiano Ricci on the staircase at Burlington House give graceful illustration of his ability (*Ill. 33*).

As might be expected, English painters were slow to return to the mural painting of which they had long lost the tradition. They were not attuned to the Baroque style, ideologically or technically. Robert Streeter (or Streater) (1624–80), who was noted in his own time for the range of his art and painted the semi-topographical and semi-narrative picture *Boscobel and Whiteladies* commemorating Charles II's escape and concealment after the battle of Worcester, seems a tyro in the decorative work by which he is principally known, the ceiling of the Sheldonian Theatre, Oxford (*Ill. 31*). His projection of figures in space falls short of the characteristic Baroque accomplishment. It is all the more remarkable that Pellegrini and the Riccis should have been followed by an Englishman who produced the most impressive work of any. This was Sir James Thornhill (1675/6–1734), whose series of paintings for the Painted Hall of what is now the Royal Naval College, Greenwich, completed in 1727, is one of the largest decorative schemes ever undertaken and a masterpiece of coherent design (*Ill. 32*).

In patriotic or chauvinistic terms Thornhill might be described as the first native painter to score a signal victory

31 Robert Streeter's ceiling of the Sheldonian Theatre, an allegory of the Arts and Sciences, with Truth as a central figure, dismissing Envy, Rapine, and Ignorance, is of interest as an English effort in Baroque decoration, though with the shortcomings that might be expected in a form of art so little cultivated in England. Streeter was admired in his own time as a 'universal' artist, practising wall and ceiling painting, landscape, still-life, and engraving

over the foreign invaders. He learnt something from Verrio and Laguerre, though more probably from actual travel in France and the direct study of Le Brun, while, through engravings, he was acquainted with the work of such Italian masters of ceiling painting as Pietro da Cortona and Andrea Pozzo. In early middle age, already successful in decorative commissions, he was chosen to paint the dome of St Paul's, the claims of the continental artists being set aside, both in this instance and for decorative projects at Hampton Court. The Riccis, worsted in competition, left England in 1716. Thornhill now had a clear field; his monochrome paintings of scenes from St Paul's life for the Cathedral were completed in 1717 and meanwhile he was working on the scheme for Greenwich, the ceiling of the Lower Hall—*The Triumph of Peace and Liberty*, an apotheosis of William and Mary, and *The Return of the*

32 This detail from the Painted Hall at Greenwich is part of the most ambitious and successful schemes of decoration to be carried out in England. It reveals Sir James Thornhill's close study and intelligent application of the Baroque style in both its treatment of space and the elaborate symbolism with which it celebrates the triumph of William and Mary. The array of symbols and symbolic figures gives due prominence to the maritime aspect of England's strength and Thornhill showed a singular ability in relating contemporary matter to an allegorical scheme of design without loss of decorative magnificence

33 The English period of the Venetian decorative painters, Pellegrini and the Riccis, is indicative of the trend of cultivated taste in the country, illustrated by Sebastiano Ricci's wall paintings in Burlington House

Golden Age of the West Wall, pointing to the promise of the Hanoverian era. Thornhill was a man of inventive mind, which shows itself in the elaborate symbolism of virtues and vices, science and the arts, and national prowess which he welded together in harmony. His numerous drawings convey the vitality of his imagination. Painting in oil on the wall plaster, in a method that the cleaning of 1960 elucidated, he and his assistants produced a work which even now a national diffidence as regards the English capacity for grandeur in art underestimates. He well deserves the praise of George Vertue as 'the greatest History painter this kingdom has produced' and the more moderate but expert assessment of Hogarth, who described the Greenwich works as 'well-invented and full of learning'.

Sir Godfrey Kneller (1646–1723), born in Lübeck, his name originally being Gottfried Kniller, invites comparison from one point of view with Lely, whom he followed as court painter. He was trained in Holland under Rembrandt's pupil Ferdinand

34, 35 The work of Sir Godfrey Kneller gives an increased value to portraiture as a record of men of literature, science, and architecture, such as *Sir Christopher Wren* of 1711 (*left*). The *Portrait of Tonson* of 1717 (*right*) is from the series depicting members of the Kit-Cat Club

Bol, settled in England in 1674 after some Italian experience, and was continuously active as a portrait painter in five reigns, those of Charles II, James II, William and Mary, Anne, and George I. Some traces of the Van Dyck-Lely tradition remain in his work and as with Lely his immense output and employment of a host of assistants made for superficiality and a mechanical finish. Yet as an artist he is quite distinct, his work being marked by a sober dignity and directness of statement. Though he favoured a certain pomp of drapery, his delineation of character has an essential simplicity which brings us somewhat nearer than before to Hogarth. If the royal portraits are often dull and formal his paintings of the creative spirits of his time are fittingly perceptive, as in his portraits of Isaac Newton and Christopher Wren (*Ill. 34*), of Dryden and Prior. A new physiognomical problem incites him to so original a result as the portrait of Michael Alphonsus Shen-Fu-Tsung, '*The Chinese Convert*' (*Ill. 36*). The uniform full wig and smooth features of Augustan notabilities are something of a mask for

36 In this *Portrait of Michael Alphonsus Shen-Fu-Tsung* 'The Chinese Convert', painted for James II in 1687, which Kneller considered his best work, it can be seen how little he depended on conventions of style

character in his celebrated series of members of the Kit-Cat Club, Whig politicians, and men of letters, but the bookseller Jacob Tonson who commissioned them is vividly portrayed in less formal aspect (*Ill. 35*).

With Kneller's contemporary the Swedish painter Michael Dahl (1656–1743), who was born and trained in Stockholm and died in London at the age of eighty-seven, the long roll of naturalized or acclimatized foreigners is almost at an end. A lesser artist than Kneller, he represents a transitional aspect of portraiture in his straightforward rendering of feature and slightly incongruous elegance of pose and gesture which seems borrowed from French example. Both characteristics

37 The chief rival of Kneller, Michael Dahl, had considerable powers of characterization as is shown by this *Self-Portrait*. Painted in 1691 after a stay in Italy, the artist's gesture towards a sculptured head may indicate his admiration for or aspiration towards classic standards

appear in his *Self-Portrait* of 1691 (*Ill. 37*). Dahl lived long enough to be respected in a new age as the doyen of an earlier School. By the reign of George II, however, the native English painter was becoming a more distinct and confident figure. The master and pupil relation links Jonathan Richardson (1665–1745), Thomas Hudson (1701–79) (*Ill. 38*), and Joshua Reynolds (1723–92). Richardson, the pupil of Riley, is still one of those minor painters whose moderate gifts were obscured by the more accomplished and assertive art of those who came from abroad, but his writings mark awareness of thought as the complement to the practice of a craft, in which there is some indication of the growth of independence. His *Theory of*

Painting was a work which stimulated the intelligence and curiosity of the young Reynolds. A national attitude to art is implicit in the idea of a training-ground for English painters, a school freely open to those with talent. The idea, shared by a number of painters at the beginning of the eighteenth century, was put into practice by Kneller and Thornhill in anticipation of the Royal Academy. Even so, the advent of so great and independent an artist as William Hogarth is a surprising phenomenon. With him the curtain rises on a changed prospect.

38 The unaffected directness of eighteenth-century portraiture begins to appear in the paintings of Thomas Hudson, the master of Sir Joshua Reynolds, as in this *Portrait of the Duchess of Buccleuch*, the second wife of the 2nd Duke of Buccleuch, painted in 1755

CHAPTER FOUR

Hogarth and his age

William Hogarth (1697–1764) was unquestionably one of the
greatest of English artists and a man of remarkably individual
character and thought. It was his achievement to give a comprehensive view of social life within the framework of
moralistic and dramatic narrative, this creation of a world
being far more important than the system of ethics or the tale
involved. He produced portraits which brought a fresh vitality
and truth into the jaded profession of what he called 'phizmongering'. He observed both high life and low with a keen
and critical eye and his range of observation was accompanied
by an exceptional capacity for dramatic composition, and in
painting by a technical quality which adds beauty to pictures
containing an element of satire or caricature.

A small stocky man with blunt pugnacious features and
alert blue eyes, he had all the sharp-wittedness of the born
Cockney and an insular pride which led to his vigorous attacks
on the exaggerated respect for foreign artists and the taste of
would-be connoisseurs who brought over (as he said) 'ship-
loads of dead Christs, Madonnas and Holy Families' by inferior
hands. There is no reason to suppose he had anything but
respect for the great Italian masters, though he deliberately
took a provocative attitude. What he objected to as much as
anything was the absurd veneration of the darkness produced
by time and varnish as well as the assumption that English
painters were necessarily inferior to others. A forthrightness of
statement may perhaps be related to his North-country

inheritance, for his father came to London from Westmorland, but was in any case the expression of a democratic outlook and unswervingly honest intelligence.

The fact that he was apprenticed as a boy to a silver-plate engraver has a considerable bearing on Hogarth's development. It instilled a decorative sense which is never absent from his most realistic productions. It introduced him to the world of prints, after famous masters or by the satirical commentators of an earlier day. Thus his early satirical engravings – on the South Sea Bubble and in parody of the paintings of William Kent (whose would-be grandiose efforts were fair game) – are in the spirit of the Dutch satirical engravings which already had a number of imitators in England. It is supposed that his painting of *The March of the Guards towards Finchley in the year 1745* was suggested by a print of Watteau's *Le Départ de Garnison*. It is the engraver's sense of line coupled with a regard for the value of Rococo curvature which governs his essay on aesthetics, *The Analysis of Beauty*.

As a painter Hogarth may be assumed to have learned the craft in Thornhill's 'academy', though his freshness of colour and feeling for the creamy substance of oil paint suggest more acquaintance than he admitted to with the technique of his French contemporaries. His first success as a painter was in the 'conversation pieces' in which his bent as an artist found a logical beginning. These informal groups of family and friends surrounded by the customary accessories of their day-to-day life were congenial in permitting him to treat a picture as a stage. He was not the inventor of the genre, which can be traced back to Dutch and Flemish art of the seventeenth century and in which he had contemporary rivals. Many were produced when he was about thirty and soon after he made his clandestine match with Thornhill's daughter in 1729, when extra efforts to gain a livelihood became necessary. With many felicities of detail and arrangement they show Hogarth still in a restrained and decorous mood. A step nearer to the comprehensive view of life was the picture of an actual stage, the

39 Hogarth's magnificent powers of composition are nowhere more fully displayed than in this spirited *Orgy* from *The Rake's Progress*, *c.* 1732. Sharp contrasts of light and dark emphasize its drama and it is possible to trace in the arrangement of the figures an application of the 'serpentine line' of Hogarth's aesthetic theory

scene from *The Beggar's Opera* with which he scored a great success about 1730, making several versions of the painting. Two prospects must have been revealed to him as a result, the idea of constructing his own pictorial drama comprising various scenes of social life, and that of reaching a wider public through the means of engraving. The first successful series *The Harlot's Progress*, of which only the engravings now exist, was immediately followed by the tremendous verve and riot of *The Rake's Progress*, *c.* 1732 (*Ill. 39*); the masterpiece of the story series the *Marriage-à-la-Mode* (*Ill. 40*) followed after an interval of twelve years.

40 The first scene of the *Marriage-à-la-Mode* (1744) shows all the sense of theatre with which Hogarth sets his stage and establishes the satirical key of his drama in four acts. Interior and figures are fascinating simply as a pictorial spectacle, but the picture is full also of clues to its story and satire, e.g. the vanity of the old nobleman (whose unfinished mansion is seen through the window) and the mutual indifference of bride and bridegroom

As a painter of social life, Hogarth shows the benefit of the system of memory training which he made a self-discipline. London was his universe and he displayed his mastery in painting every aspect of its people and architecture, from the mansion in Arlington Street, the interior of which provided the setting for the disillusioned couple in the second scene of the *Marriage-à-la-Mode*, to the dreadful aspect of Bedlam. Yet he was not content with one line of development only and the work of his mature years takes a varied course. He could not

41 In *O the Roast Beef of Old England!* (*Calais Gate*) of 1748, Hogarth displayed his intention of conveying 'to my countrymen the striking difference between the food, priests, soldiers, etc. of two nations so contiguous that in a clear day one coast may be seen from the other'. Yet besides insularity of comment it contains passages of painting as admirable in themselves as the distant religious procession seen beneath the portcullis

resist the temptation to attempt a rivalry with the history painters, though with little success. The Biblical compositions for St Bartholomew's Hospital on which he embarked after *The Rake's Progress* were not of a kind to convey his real genius. He is sometimes satirical as in *The March of the Guards towards Scotland*, and the *O the Roast Beef of Old England!* (*Calais Gate*) (*Ill. 41*), which was a product of his single expedition abroad with its John Bull comment on the condition of France, and also the 'Election' series of 1755 with its richness of

61

42 Hogarth painted the children of Daniel Graham, Apothecary to Chelsea Hospital, in 1742, in the most engaging of his conversation pieces, notable for its play of expression and movement and for the freshness and delicacy of its colour

comedy. In portraiture he displays a great variety. The charm of childhood, the ability to compose a vivid group, a delightful delicacy of colour appear in *The Graham Children* of 1742 (*Ill. 42*). The portrait heads of his servants (*Ill. 43*) are penetrating studies of character. The painting of Captain Coram, the philanthropic sea captain who took a leading part in the foundation of the Foundling Hospital, adapts the formality of

43 Hogarth only objected to what he called 'phizmongering' in so far as this implied slavish obedience to a patron's dictates. His enjoyment of portraiture at a democratic level is evident in this very English group of *c.* 1782. Unfinished and not formally composed, it was no doubt intended as a household record only and remained in Mrs Hogarth's possession at their Chiswick house until the sale of her effects in 1790. Here is character without a trace of caricature

the ceremonial portrait to a democratic level with a singularly engaging effect. The quality of Hogarth as an artist is seen to advantage in his sketches and one sketch in particular, the famous *Shrimp Girl* quickly executed with a limited range of colour, stands alone in his work, taking its place among the masterpieces of the world in its harmony of form and content, its freshness and vitality.

Hogarth's true painter's gift has in the past been somewhat obscured by the subject interest which equally appears in the engravings (Charles Lamb in his essay on 'The Genius of Hogarth' makes no distinction between engravings and paintings). It has also been obscured by the literary, moral, satirical, and humorous complications attendant on his professed aim of emulating the dramatic writer. Yet his truly creative spirit outweighs any aesthetic cavils to which these complications might give rise. To broaden the view of art in such a way as to take in the whole of social life was a great and fruitful effort.

The genius of Hogarth is such that he is often regarded as a solitary rebel against a decaying artificiality, and yet, though he had no pupils, he had contemporaries who, while of lesser stature in one way and another, tended in the same direction. There are the several practitioners of the conversation piece, introduced into England about 1725 by the French painter Philip Mercier but popularized and nationalized by Hogarth. Among them is Joseph Highmore (1692–1780), some of whose paintings have been attributed to Hogarth himself, a delightful artist who until quite recent times has received far less attention than he deserves. A Londoner by birth, trained in Kneller's 'academy' in Great Queen Street and a founder-member of the later academy in St Martin's Lane where Hogarth seems to have presided occasionally and unconventionally, Highmore may be associated with Hogarth in terms of friendship and as a fellow-contributor to the scheme which provided the Foundling Hospital with a series of history pictures. He is, however, more distinguished for the illustrations to Samuel Richardson which to some extent provide a parallel with Hogarth's scenes of social life, though different inasmuch as Highmore was not inventing but following the episodes described in the novelist's text. Now distributed between the National Gallery of Victoria, the Fitzwilliam Museum, and the Tate Gallery, the illustrations to *Pamela* (*Ill. 44*) are admirable studies of eighteenth-century life, lacking in Hogarth's inimitable power but with a refinement and

44 The graceful style of Joseph Highmore is characteristically represented in the illustrations to Richardson's *Pamela* of which this painting of *c.* 1744 is one. The delicacy of his style is in contrast with the robust products of Hogarth's genius, though examples of his work, little studied until recent times, have been confused with those of Hogarth

delicacy to which the influence of the French engraver Hubert Gravelot, who worked in London between 1732 and 1745, may have contributed.

A naturalism akin to that of Hogarth but distinct in its delicate charm appears in the illustration to *Clarissa Harlowe*, long attributed to the greater master. In portraiture Highmore was capable not only of the charm which distinguishes his female portraits but of such a study of masculine character as his group of *Mr Oldham and his Guests*, now in the Tate

45 Francis Hayman's *Family Group*, *c*. 1745, is a good example of the conversation piece in which the personal relation of the sitters is emphasized by the pictorial links of composition. The elegance of composition and figures suggests the influence of the French engraver, Hubert Gravelot

Gallery. This jovial group so delicately observed was also mistakenly given to Hogarth for a long period and made its entry obscurely into the Tate Gallery as 'British School, Eighteenth Century' though the evidence of style proclaims it Highmore at his best.

Francis Hayman (1708–76) is another painter of merit in Hogarth's circle. He accompanied him on the trip to France which produced *Calais Gate* and was with him in Moll King's tavern when the spectacle of a woman spitting gin at her rival suggested to Hogarth the incident he painted in the orgy scene in *The Rake's Progress*. Hayman was respected in his own time as a history painter and seems to have been trained by Robert Brown, a pupil of Thornhill. He is now remembered, however, by conversation pieces in which he followed Hogarth, depicting a sedate middle class in a simple domestic setting (*Ill. 45*). He is also noted for his decorations for the

46 Like Hayman, Arthur Devis was a prolific and accomplished painter of conversation pieces. Groups with a landscape background, such as this picture (1751) of the Secretary of the East India Company and his family, may have contributed to Gainsborough's adoption of this open-air genre

Supper Boxes of the Vauxhall pleasure gardens, a scheme to which Hogarth contributed, remaining examples of which are to be found in the Victoria and Albert Museum and Tate Gallery. Like Highmore, he seems to have been influenced by the French engraver Gravelot and to have derived from him the style of open-air conversation piece which contained the promise of further development. Hayman's paintings of country gentlemen taking their ease in a rural setting, beneath a foreground tree with a distant landscape prospect behind, seem already to anticipate the early masterpieces of Gainsborough and may well have had a direct influence on the latter, who had some association as a student in London with both Gravelot and Hayman.

Arthur Devis (1711–87) is another delightful painter of the middle-class conversation piece (*Ill. 46*), like Hayman cultivating especially the open-air setting and in the unpretentious simplicity of his style once again emphasizing the new spirit animating portraiture in the age of George II. The conversation piece indeed remained throughout the century a style of informal composition productive of happy results, though in the person of Joshua Reynolds we once again find English painting attempting to rise to a grander level and resuming the contact with the continental tradition from which Hogarth had declared his independence. It was Reynolds's aim to raise the status of English art not, in Hogarth's fashion, by insular defiance but by a superiority of knowledge and ambition.

It seems a necessary part of his destiny that after a period spent as pupil of the portrait painter Thomas Hudson, Reynolds as a young man should have had the chance of visiting Italy and in a stay of over three years acquired that acquaintance with the works of the great Italian masters, in Rome mainly but also in Venice, which played so large a part in the formation of his philosophy of art and, in some degree, of his style. It seems equally a matter of destiny that in the years of success and prestige which followed his return to London the idea of an Academy, so long discussed, should at last find fruition and royal acknowledgement and that it should provide the incentive to give his thoughts on art a precise literary form. To understand his outlook it is necessary to refer, not only to his paintings but to the *Discourses* which as first President of the Royal Academy he addressed to the students year by year, constructing an orderly philosophic system, establishing a hierarchy of great masters and extracting from their example the essential qualities of the 'Grand Style'.

The argument, with its insistence on the general as opposed to the particular, the need to correct the accidents and 'particularities' of nature and to profit by the example of the masters of the Italian Renaissance, was the reverse of Hogarth's ideas and an implicit criticism of his art. How did Reynolds apply it in his own painting? As he was primarily a portrait painter, one might conclude that much of his exposition of the Grand Style was irrelevant. History painting of a religious or classical kind was as much outside his scope as that of Hogarth. Reynolds indeed had many English traits which his principles would deprecate – a humour for instance which appears in some caricature portraits executed in Rome, and, though early corrected, is still discernible in such a work as his *Garrick between Comedy and Tragedy*; a strong sense of individual character; a sentiment which appears in his pictures of children.

He was, however, able to assemble from European precedent not from Italian masters alone (and certainly not from Michelangelo whom he admired most of all), but from Rembrandt, Rubens, Van Dyck, and the Venetians, a style which had a grandeur of its own. It is well exemplified in the truly majestic *Self-Portrait* (*Ill. 47*), in which he stands, in the robes of a DCL, the degree conferred on him by Oxford in 1773, by a bust of Michelangelo. The conception is deliberately based, not on Italian models but on Rembrandt's *Aristotle contemplating the bust of Homer*.

In the richness of colour inspired by great European models, Reynolds is outstanding, not only in mellow warmth such as pervades the portrait of Lord Heathfield but in a flexible variety as may be seen in the delicacies of blue and grey to be found in the delightful *Nelly O'Brien* (*Ill. 48*). A technical carelessness and an experimental desire for a heightened richness, led him to use bitumen, that radio-active pitch which has darkened and ruined some of his works, but those unaffected show him as a subtle and masterly colourist.

The Grand Style element in Reynolds's portraiture sometimes gives the impression of a theatrical or even playful adjunct, as in the group of the Montgomery sisters as *Three Ladies adorning a Term of Hymen* (*Ill. 49*). It is refined, however, into an atmosphere of distinction in the magnificent series of single figures in which, more than any other painter, he gives a personal history of his age and such a survey of English character as no one since Holbein had been able to realize. He has impressed on the mind of later times the characteristic image of illustrious contemporaries, Dr Johnson, Laurence

47 This magnificent *Self-Portrait*, probably painted soon after Reynolds became a DCL of Oxford in 1773, is almost a profession of artistic faith and learning. Its treatment declares his attachment to Titian and Rembrandt and the bust beside him, to Michelangelo

Sterne, Oliver Goldsmith, Gibbon, Burke, Fox, Garrick, Mrs Siddons. In his paintings of children he is entirely natural and unaffected. When all is said and done, it is informality to which he tended in his later work and not a rigidity of doctrine.

The tendency to look once more to the continent of Europe can be seen in the work of the Scottish painter Allan Ramsay (1713–84), long neglected but now recognized as one who made an original contribution to the classic age of portraiture. Like Reynolds, Ramsay spent some years in Italy but unlike him was not mainly affected by the masters of the great past or inclined to base any formal system on their study. What impressed him was the elegance of the contemporary Italian painters, the Neapolitan decorative artist Francesco Solimena, and Pompeo Batoni who produced so many charming pictures of aristocratic English visitors to Rome. He returned to England from his first Italian visit in 1738 and thanks to the grace

48 Painted in 1763, Reynolds's *Portrait of Nelly O'Brien*, a well-known beauty of the time, is a masterpiece in which lighting, colour, and material textures show the artist's technique at its best before he embarked on his efforts to emulate Rembrandt in richness and depth of dark tones. There is even an effect of open-air light, rare for the period

49 *Three Ladies adorning a Term of Hymen*, a portrait group with an admixture of classical fancy, depicting the three daughters of Sir William Montgomery, which Reynolds painted in 1773 at Luke Gardiner's request for 'an emblematic or historical subject'. Gardiner was then engaged to Elizabeth Montgomery, the centre figure in the picture

and ease of his art his work was soon much in demand. He may be considered secondary to Hogarth in having introduced a new informality into portraiture, but he was able to popularize it with those fashionable circles from which Hogarth stubbornly remained aloof. In middle age he seems to have been freshly inspired by French contemporaries, Quentin de la Tour and Nattier and then to have vied with Reynolds, ten years his junior. The exceptional beauty of his portraits of women, in which Horace Walpole considered that he excelled Reynolds, can be seen in the portrait of his second wife,

Margaret Lindsay (*Ill. 51*) with its pastel-like delicacy of colour and sweetness of expression. His *Lady Mary Coke* (*Ill. 50*) painted in 1762 is a masterly full-length of his best period. Soon after, his work showed a falling-off, partly because of the output demanded of him and partly no doubt because his delicate vein of talent was exhausted. Yet, although he was without Reynolds's variety or masculine force Ramsay was a painter of incomparable charm.

50 Eighteenth-century portraiture reached its height in the 1760s, and Allan Ramsay's full-length *Portrait of Lady Mary Coke*, painted in 1762, is a superb example. She holds a seventeenth-century theorbo and in the grace of pose and treatment of the dress Ramsay seems to have Van Dyck in mind

51 This *Portrait of Margaret Lindsay*, Ramsay's second wife, *c.* 1755, fragrant in charm, shows the mastery of style he had perfected by continental study. Here as in a number of other paintings, he set himself the problem of harmoniously relating head and out-stretched hand

The art of Thomas Gainsborough (1727–88) is in striking contrast with that of either Hogarth or Reynolds. These two were essentially townsmen; by affection as well as birth Gainsborough was a countryman. His art was aristocratic, that is to say it tended towards an ideal, in which respect it clearly differed from the realistic outlook of Hogarth the 'man of the people'. Hogarth's view of life was bounded by London and though the 'Election' series has its admirable landscape backgrounds they are incidental to the human action, whereas Gainsborough found his greatest satisfaction in landscape composition in which the figures were, in his own words, 'such as fill a place (I won't say stop a Gap) or to create a little business for the Eye to be drawn from the Trees in order to return to them with more glee'.

To say that his tendency was towards an ideal might seem to place him in close accord with Reynolds, yet a wide difference at once appears between the consciously formed intellectual attitude of Reynolds, with its reference to the greatness of Italy, and the free and instinctive fashion in which Gainsborough sought to 'deliver' as he said 'a fine sentiment'. It is significant that Reynolds spent some years in Italy and Gainsborough was never tempted to leave his native land. Under the pressure of contemporary patronage he was 'chiefly in the Face way', though in spite of his success as a portrait painter he has left no such gallery of the illustrious, observed with intense psychological interest, as Reynolds provides. He excels with the type rather than the individual and most of all in visions of beauty and grace. In his painting portraiture, landscape, and the art of imaginative composition are uniquely found together. In the sense that his work presents an analogy with poetry and music which is absent from that of Hogarth and Reynolds he has the advantage of both.

In its formation Gainsborough's art seems to stem from various sources. The period spent in his teens in London with the French engraver Hubert Gravelot (before the latter left for Paris in 1745) must have given him a feeling for the delicacy

of the French pastoral, though Hayman, who comes within
the same ambience and whom the young Gainsborough certainly knew, provides a direct antecedent for the open-air
conversation piece in which Gainsborough's mastery was
beautifully shown in his Suffolk period at Sudbury and
Ipswich. The pose of *John Plampin of Chadacre* (*Ill. 52*) reclining by a tree, with one of those dogs Gainsborough always
painted so well, is very similar to that of Hayman's *Garrick and
Wyndham*. How far the genius of Gainsborough transcended
such models is, however, shown by the superb *Mr and Mrs Robert
Andrews* (*Ill. 53*), so sentient in every respect of English
country and English life.

The taste of the time for Dutch pictures and the affinity
between Holland and East Anglia give an indication of his
starting-point in landscape. He had some experience in copying
and restoring paintings by Ruisdael and others. How well he
adapted and transformed the Dutch method of composition

52, 53, 54 Gainsborough's attachment to his native East Anglia is manifest in
these early works: *John Plampin of Chadacre* (1755) (*above opposite*), and *Mr and Mrs
Robert Andrews* (1748–9) (*below opposite*). *Cornard Wood* (or *Gainsborough's Forest*)
(*below*) seems to have been painted in 1748

55 In *The Painter's Daughters with a Cat* of *c.* 1758, and in all studies of his small daughters, Gainsborough displayed both a sympathy with childhood, always pronounced in English painting, and a freshness and simplicity of style in which he was altogether original

is shown in the magnificent *Cornard Wood* (*Ill. 54*). A freshness in which there is both a feeling for country life and a sense of the charm of immaturity is revealed in the paintings of his small daughters (*Ill. 55*), probably executed at Ipswich before he set out for Bath and the second phase of his career.

During his fourteen years at Bath (1759–74) his success as a fashionable portrait painter gave his work a new direction. He was now influenced by Van Dyck whose paintings he was able to appreciate at Wilton and in other great houses. As a result his portraits took on a new elegance and subtlety of technique (*Ill. 56*). From the 1760s onwards it appears in many masterpieces and his style reaches its perfection in his last period, in London from 1744 to 1788, *The Morning Walk* (*Ill. 57*) being a superb example.

56 Intended to be 'the completest of pictures', this *Portrait of the Hon. Mrs Graham* (1775–6), which occupied Gainsborough for a year, marks the change of style due to the influence of Van Dyck. The same young woman appears in the simple garb of Gainsborough's *The Housemaid* (Tate Gallery)

In the landscape for which in these city years Gainsborough constantly expressed a nostalgic preference he makes a like departure. It is sometimes lamented that an authentic Suffolk no longer appears in his work, though the assumption that landscape was simply an atrophied memory may well be discounted. He was evidently more concerned than before with general principles of massing and lighting as in the magnificent *Market Cart*, c. 1786–7 (Tate Gallery). It was in harmony with this generalizing tendency that the human figures became Arcadian peasants rather than local rustics. His habit of making miniature landscapes in the studio out of odd scraps of vegetable and mineral matter and his delight in the dramatic entertainment called the 'Eidophusikon' which caused him to invent his own peepshow box, in which transparencies lit by the flicker of candles gave a rich variety of effect, are aspects of his experimental interest in both form and light and shade.

Technically, Gainsborough was most original both in portraits and landscape. Those 'odd scratches and marks . . . this chaos which by a kind of magic at a certain distance assumes form', on which Reynolds commented with a mixture of disapproval and admiration, was a brilliant way of animating a surface. He seems very 'modern' in his drawings and the combination of different media which makes many of them a species of free painting. Opaque and transparent colour are sometimes found together; sometimes he lays a transparent wash over a chalk ground, working further over the surface with touches of chalk or body colour or using chalk, pen, and brush over an opaque foundation, frequently varnishing the drawing to add something of the richness of oil, dabbing in broad touches (his 'moppings') with a sponge tied to the end of a stick and as a result producing extraordinary impressions of light and substance.

57 This marriage portrait, *The Morning Walk*, painted in 1785, represents the perfection of Gainsborough's later style and goes beyond portraiture to an ideal conception of dignity and grace in the harmony of landscape and figures

Gainsborough's love of experiment and his entirely personal quest of the ideal took various directions, especially marked in his later years. It is to be noted that his affection for his native Suffolk and its lowland country did not prevent him from seeking the 'sublime' in the Lake District in the 1780s. The 'fancy pictures' as he termed the imaginative compositions of his final period, though few of them are left, include such an original production as the *Diana and Actaeon* (*Ill. 58*) of the Royal Collection. Although he remarked, with humorous envy, on Reynolds's variety, he was in fact much the more varied of the two. Reynolds remarked that Gainsborough 'did not look at Nature with a poet's eye', by which he meant, perhaps, in a literary fashion. On the contrary, if one defines the poetry of a painter as an imaginative view of his world, investing it with rhythmic grace, Gainsborough was the most poetic artist of this great age.

58 *Diana and Actaeon*, a 'fancy picture' left unfinished at Gainsborough's death, shows him in the process of developing a new and imaginative mode of expression which if he had lived might well have become one of the most remarkable aspects of his art. It is a reminder of the fact that he never ceased to progress and that he was able to transcend the routine of professional portraiture

CHAPTER FIVE

Early phases of landscape and topography

When Gainsborough died in 1788 the entrance hall of Schom-
berg House, Pall Mall, where he lived, was lined with unsold
landscapes, a fact which emphasizes that in this aspect of his
art he was somewhat isolated and unappreciated. To some
extent, however, the ground was already prepared for the great
expansion of the art of landscape by painters of rather earlier
date and activity. Their work has some relation to the trend
of English taste and the rising popularity of the Grand Tour,
which had instilled so great a regard for the classical landscapes of Claude and the souvenir of Italy which a Canaletto
could provide. In a sense this was an aspect of the connoisseurship deplored by Hogarth which ignored the native painters,
though the latter in the first half of the eighteenth century
found a market for marine and topographical views. The
marine painters followed in the steps of Willem van de Velde
the Younger and form an attractive minor 'School'. They
include Peter Monamy (c. 1670–1749), examples of whose
work, e.g. *A Calm* (Dulwich Gallery) have been attributed to
the Dutch master; Charles Brooking (1723–59) who painted
shipping, marine views, and sea fights after the Dutch manner;
and Dominic Serres (1722–93) who became marine painter to
George III (*Ill. 59*). The principal artist in this vein is Samuel
Scott, who died in 1772 at about the age of seventy. Beginning with an ambition to paint ships and sea fights like Van
de Velde, as time went on he became celebrated for those
views of London which earned him the title of the 'English

59 *The Relief of Gibraltar* of *c*. 1781 by Dominic Serres, a Gascon by birth, who was taken prisoner in 1758 when master of a trading vessel and brought to England. He took up painting and exhibited sea pieces from 1761, becoming a foundation-member of the Royal Academy in 1768. He received some assistance in his early efforts from Charles Brooking, an employee in the dockyard at Deptford, also of note in the history of English marine painting

Canaletto'. He collaborated with George Lambert (1710–65), an artist whose merits have only recently received attention, in a series of six paintings illustrating the ports and settlements of the East India Company (now in the Ministry of Commonwealth Relations), but he seems to have concentrated on London from about 1735 and to have been painting the Thames (*Ill. 62*) from London Bridge to Westminster some years before Canaletto came from Venice to paint the same themes. As well as possessing great topographical interest Scott's views of the city are beautifully painted in a style distinguishable from that of Canaletto, though no doubt deriving some stimulus from the Venetian artist, who worked in England from 1746 to 1756.

84

Canaletto had an English pupil in William James, whose paintings of London are sometimes confused with those of Scott. Canaletto's influence, however, was not entirely topographical. His fluent brushwork may have had its suggestion for Hogarth and his sense of space and light for Richard Wilson, who ascends beyond topography (though this played a minor part in his work) into a far broader conception of landscape. Wilson (1714–82) was mainly a portrait painter until he was thirty-five. He then visited Italy (Venice, Rome, Naples) and was encouraged by the advice of Zuccarelli and Joseph Vernet to devote himself to landscape painting. His subsequent career, though unattended by material success, was a magnificent addition to English art.

An ostensible model for Wilson was the 'classical' landscape of Claude Lorrain and Gaspard Poussin though he seems to have equally admired the glowing effects of light obtained by Cuyp and to have borrowed something of the Dutch style of

60 The ascent of landscape beyond topography can be appreciated in the breadth and simplicity of design of this painting of *Mount Snowdon* by Wilson

61, 62 Wilson's view of the *River Dee near Eaton Hall* (*above*) shows in what admirable fashion he made use in England of lessons learned in Italy as to the importance of light. His characteristic method of painting against the sun so that the foliage is tipped with its sparkle is a decided factor in the effect. *Entrance to the Fleet River* (*right*) (*c.* 1750) is by Samuel Scott, who first became of note as a marine painter, and began to draw and paint topographical subjects along the Thames about 1735. He is sometimes referred to as the 'English Canaletto', and his London views are parallel in aim with Canaletto's, though distinct in style

treating foliage. Yet a principal influence on him was Italy itself and its light and geological structure. A strong individuality appears not only in his capacity to envelop a picture in luminous atmosphere but in breadth of construction and arrangement of masses without the intrusion of irrelevant details or ideas. As Reynolds remarked, 'his landscape was in reality too near common nature to admit supernatural objects' (i.e. the gods and goddesses, nymphs and fauns in which the connoisseur delighted), but this criticism only underlines his true merit.

In terms of place, Wilson's landscape has three phases: the views of Southern Italy (often repeated after his return to England, sometimes in versions of inferior quality); views in the region of London and along the Thames and of English country-houses (*Ill. 61*); and finally views of the mountain scenery of his native Wales. In each he produced memorable

visions of light and space with, also, a powerful simplicity of design which can be fully appreciated in his paintings of Snowdon (*Ill. 60*) and mountain lakes. Ruskin's belief that 'with the name of Richard Wilson, the history of sincere landscape art founded on a meditative love of nature begins in England' does this great artist no more than justice. Certainly his fellow-artists and successors in landscape appreciated his achievement though the connoisseurs remained indifferent. He had a number of immediate followers, George Barret (1728–84) who imitated his style, William Hodges (1744–97) his studio-assistant, William Marlow (1740–1813), Thomas Wright (active early nineteenth century), Wilson's first biographer. If these are minor figures, the important fact remains that Wilson 'opened the way to the genuine principles of landscape in England' and inspired that succession in which the illustrious names of Constable and Turner stand out.

CHAPTER SIX

Rural life and sport

The great increase of country-houses in the eighteenth century, under a settled rule and in settled conditions, the rise of a squirearchy, the improvement of agriculture, the development of a rural routine of sport were productive of a genre closely allied to landscape but distinct in giving prominence to rural activity. Horse-racing, revived in the latter part of the seventeenth century, became organized with the foundation of the Jockey Club about 1750. Fox-hunting as a chase on horseback seems to have made its appearance about the beginning of the eighteenth century (before then, foxes were shot or trapped). They produced a demand for sporting pictures of a kind popular until well into the nineteenth century.

The primitives of the genre were John Wootton (c. 1682–1765), Pieter Tillemans (1684–1734), and James Seymour (1702–52). Tillemans, born in Antwerp, who came to England in 1708, worked in the vein of Teniers and painted both sporting scenes and views of country-seats. Seymour, more particularly a specialist in horse portraiture, was naïve and hard in style, not undecorative, but without great pretensions as an artist. Wootton best conveys the spirit of rural recreation in the peaceful era of Sir Robert Walpole. The pupil of Jan Wyck, he replaced the battlefields of his master by the hunting-field. He had a feeling for landscape which he studied in the works of Claude and Gaspard Poussin; this is evident in his background, though his borrowed conventions of rocks and trees were regarded with contempt by John Constable. He

63 Wootton's *Members of the Beaufort Hunt* (1744) is a notable effort to create a picture as well as a document of sport. This appears in the care he has devoted to a natural grouping of figures and animals and also to the landscape setting. Though the landscape shows his debt to Claude, the borrowing is discreetly made. As well as Dutch paintings, his work was probably suggestive of possibilities in landscape to the young Gainsborough

paid attention to the natural grouping of figures, by which he adds interest to the portraits of horses he painted at Newmarket. As a coherent composition, relating landscape, figures, horses, and hounds, his *Members of the Beaufort Hunt*, 1744 (*Ill. 63*), is a painting of note in the history of sporting art.

64 The natural grouping still rudimentary in Wootton becomes a triumph of composition with Stubbs. In *The Prince of Wales's Phaeton* (1793) he resolves the problem of horse portraiture by interspersing variety of incident, the human figures and the leaping dog being full of character. Details throughout are studied with attention not merely to fact but to their value of design. It may be noted how the curious structure of the carriage thus takes on pictorial interest related to that of the horses' trappings. As always Stubbs is keenly aware of the expressiveness of silhouette

That history is on the whole a matter of specialist study rather than of aesthetic importance, yet any genre depends on the quality of those who practise it and we suddenly find one of the greatest of eighteenth-century artists rising out of this milieu in the person of George Stubbs. Stubbs (1724–1806)

65 *Gimcrack with a Groom on Newmarket Heath*, painted by Stubbs for Lord Bolingbroke, whose colours are worn by the jockey, and who was the owner of Gimcrack, is one of his masterpieces if considered simply as the disposition of objects in space. The horse appears twice in the picture, portrayed near the Rubbing House in the left foreground, and in the background winning a race, probably the event at Newmarket of 12 July 1765

was more an animal painter than a sporting painter and more of an artist in a truly creative sense than a specialist in either field. He had little formal training though he showed an interest in the construction and anatomy of the human and animal frame at an early stage of his career. He was first a portrait painter in the provinces and travelled to Italy at the age of twenty, though the miniaturist Ozias Humphry, who wrote a memoir based on conversations with Stubbs, records that he merely wished to satisfy himself that 'nature was and always is superior to Art, whether Greek or Roman' and having done so promptly returned homewards. In the fashion of the Renaissance masters who dissected human corpses in their study of anatomy, he began a study of the anatomy of the horse at Horkstrow in Lincolnshire in 1758 which culminated in the famous illustrated work published in 1766.

At about that time he was much employed by the sporting aristocracy and continued to be so during the later stages of his long life in paintings of Newmarket and pictures of horses (*Ill. 64*); yet when his work is surveyed as a whole what becomes apparent is an amazing power of imbuing whatever he depicts with a superb aesthetic quality.

A masterpiece is his *Gimcrack with a Groom, Jockey and Stable Lad on Newmarket Heath, c.* 1765 (*Ill. 65*), of which he painted more than one version. The great open stretch of sky, the precisely defined architecture of the stable-buildings, the faultless placing of the figures and horses come together into a magnificently ordered composition. No other painting of a single horse approaches in positive grandeur his *Hambletonian, Rubbing down* though here, as in other works, he establishes an exquisite relation between horse, stable-boy, and groom, the latter a living character worthy of Velazquez. His series of mares and foals (*Ill. 66*) is one of beautiful variations in their arrangement in a landscape setting.

Stubbs was also a master of the open-air conversation piece, as in the splendid group *The Melbourne and Milbanke Family* and the painting of John and Sophia Masters setting out for a ride from Colwick Hall. Rural labour inspired delightful combinations of figure and landscape, some of which were executed in a delicate technique of enamel colour on plaques provided by the potter Josiah Wedgwood. Paintings of wild animals, executed in the 1770s and later, convey an interest in the exotic in which Stubbs seems one of the Romantic pioneers. It is related that pausing at Ceuta on his way back from Italy he saw a lion devouring a horse, a scene which so impressed him that he later made a series of paintings of the subject. The terror and violence depicted in the enamel on copper of 1770 anticipate the Romantic passion expressed by Delacroix and Géricault. Yet Stubbs himself seems a man of calm detachment; the greatness of his art is that of pictorial design planned with a rational thoroughness and at the same time with the most sensitive appreciation of line and form.

66 The series of mares and foals was a beautiful product of Stubbs's art during the 1760s. The paintings were produced for aristocratic sporting patrons who no doubt wished for portraits of horses belonging to them, though it has been remarked that the same horses recur in several of the pictures and it would seem that Stubbs was mainly interested in the variations he could make upon a theme. In this example there is no element suggestive of sport nor has the artist chosen to introduce the human element; the result is a poetic vision of nature

Something of the broad outlook of Stubbs remains in Benjamin Marshall (*c.* 1767–1835) who painted many portraits of race-horses, their trainers and owners (*Ill. 67*). The sporting school now tended to become a narrowing specialization. Most productive at the end of the eighteenth and in the first half of the nineteenth century, it is of interest mainly as a record of horses and riders rather than for artistic originality, though numbering such able exponents as John Nost Sartorius (1755–1828), John Ferneley (1782–1860), John Frederick Herring (1795–1865), and Henry Alken (active 1816–31).

The rural life which Stubbs so beautifully evoked and of which Gainsborough in his later landscapes gave so ideal a version is again painted with singular charm by George Morland (1763–1804). Morland, naturally gifted, was subjected

67 *The Prince of Wales's Roan Hack*, by Benjamin Marshall, who was an able follower of Stubbs though he confined himself more specifically to horse portraiture and lacked that purely artistic genius which places Stubbs among the great eighteenth-century painters. This example of his work provides comparison

by his father, painter and picture restorer, to a severe early training which may well account for the facility he developed later. He learned by copying Dutch and Flemish masters, though Gainsborough was perhaps the greatest single influence on his work. It was due rather to the limitations of his mentality than to the Bohemian and disordered life he led that despite many admirable features his work often seems superficial. He had something of the stubborn pride and independence which caused Hogarth to rebel against the dictation of patronage. It led him to much sordid durance in garrets and sponging-houses. Nevertheless, he saw and was observant of a good deal of rural England in the still countrified environs of London, in Leicestershire and the Isle of Wight. In spite of the rough realities of his career he created an idyll, an Arcadian vision of tranquil cottagers, never, as Sickert remarked, seen at work (unlike the struggling peasants of Barbizon as seen by Millet), of picturesque farmyards and their animals which he painted with masterly skill, of domestic-looking alehouses about which cluster mild and temperate groups (*Ill. 68*). He had a command of mellow and luminous paint, delightful at its best, though too many pictures were evidently dashed off in haste to satisfy a creditor or rescue him from a sponging-house. He falls short of greatness and yet his idyll of rural life is something to which English feeling still responds.

Morland's brother-in-law James Ward (1769–1859), also an animal painter and a painter of some sporting subjects, though influenced by him in his early work must be regarded separately and in the different context of the Romantic spirit in English painting by which Morland was entirely unaffected. Nearest to Morland, indeed, are those minor genre painters of the later eighteenth century who while not necessarily devoted to rural life invest the popular life of the time with a like charm, an idyllic placidity. They include both Henry Walton (1746–1813) whose *Girl buying a Ballad* (*Ill. 69*) has this particular fragrance, and Francis Wheatley (1747–1801) who conveys it

68 Sometimes included in the category of sporting artists, George Morland is better
viewed as the painter of English rural life in its picturesque and idyllic aspect as in *Outside
the Alehouse Door* of 1792. Carefully trained by his father, the painter Henry Robert
Morland, in the study and copying of Dutch pictures, he was also in some degree a
pioneer in his clear tones and broad effects of light

69, 70 The idyllic aspect of English painting noticed in the work of Morland is also to be found in such charming minor painters as Henry Walton and Francis Wheatley. They anticipate the kind of genre painting which was later so characteristic of English middle-class taste in the nineteenth century. Apart from some details of costume, the *Girl buying a Ballad* by Walton (*left*), a pupil of Zoffany, exhibited in the Academy of 1778, might have been painted a hundred years later, while Wheatley's *Return from Market* (1786) (*right*) also foreshadows a Victorian genre

even in so metropolitan a theme as the *Cries of London* for which he has always retained a modest celebrity, or in such an attractive work as the *Return from Market* (*Ill. 70*). The Arcadian thread in English painting, sometimes tending to oversweetness, is to be reckoned with among eighteenth-century characteristics as well as the grander mood.

CHAPTER SEVEN

Portraiture in the later eighteenth century

Though Reynolds and Gainsborough were far above their contemporaries in portraiture, a certain consistency of style is to be found throughout the latter half of the century, giving to the work of lesser artists a breadth and dignity which belong to the great age. It appears in one aspect of the art of George Romney (1734–1802) though his was a divided personality and ambition led him to deviations, interesting but scarcely fortunate. At one time he seemed the third of a great trium-virate with Reynolds and Gainsborough, for a while rivalling Reynolds in popularity after he settled in London in 1762. A sober realism was his best asset and though his group of *The Beaumont Family* (*Ill. 72*) has a stiffness which betrays his lack of resource in an elaborate composition it is admirable in its sense of masculine character. He was successful in single figures to which he could give simplicity of contour and colour (*Ill. 71*). The *Lady in a Brown Dress* which used to be known as *The Parson's Daughter* is an example; and even in the 1790s, when his ability was confused and weakening, this simplicity delightfully appears in such a portrait as that of Lady Charlotte Townsend. A want of depth and substance in his art became evident after his visit to Italy in 1773–5, which filled him with dreams of excelling in classical and imaginative themes. It can be seen in many of the portraits of Lady Hamilton, whom he envisaged as the principal figure in various allegorical subject paintings. His breakdown in health and return to Kendal in 1789 left his dreams unfulfilled.

72 One of Romney's best works is his painting of the five children and the son-in-law of Richard Beaumont of Huddersfield, painted between 1777 and 1779. The composition shows some of his shortcomings as a designer; for instance, in a want of relation between the groups to left and right, while the view of a distant landscape at the left tends to divert the eye from the central incident; yet the picture admirably displays the realism which was his great asset. Freshness of colour and directness of handling add their distinction to the convincing reality of the figures

The list of accomplished portrait painters is a long one. Francis Cotes (1726–70), the pupil of George Knapton, excelled in pastel and was capable of an elegance which is well seen in his portrait of Paul Sandby (*Ill. 73*). John Hoppner (1758–1810) acquired from Reynolds a breadth of style which saves him from mediocrity and the portrait usually described as *Mrs Williams* (*Ill. 74*), engraved as *The Mob Cap*, makes an

71 The skill which made Romney a rival to Reynolds as the portraitist of fashionable society can be appreciated in this *Portrait of Lady Rodbard* of 1786. He has evidently profited a good deal by Reynolds's example in the combination of grace and stateliness which it displays

73, 74 Tradition in eighteenth-century portraiture has a special meaning in that the influence of Reynolds was strong and widespread. Among those influenced by him was the oil painter and pastellist Francis Cotes. His *Portrait of Paul Sandby* at a window overlooking Windsor Great Park (frequent subject of Sandby's watercolours) has the elegance of the period (1759) (*above*). John Hoppner, another painter influenced by Reynolds, excels in the painting presumed to be that of a *Mrs Williams* (*c.* 1790) (*opposite*), said to have been a cloakroom attendant at Covent Garden Theatre

attractive complement to Romney's *Lady in a Brown Dress*. Sturdy merits are to be found, with some defects of technique and over-emphasis on dark shadow, in the work of John Opie (1761–1807) who gained an instant success in the London of the 1780s as 'the Cornish Wonder' (*Ill. 75*).

The conversation piece, that especially English contribution to art, continued in vogue throughout the century. Johann

75 After the bold and somewhat coarsely executed paintings with which John Opie first attracted attention, he applied himself for a time to rustic subjects in which he was happily influenced by Gainsborough. Gainsborough's *Cottage Girl with Pigs* was a much praised exhibit at the Academy of 1782, and it seems probable that Opie was inspired by it to paint *The Peasant's Family* in *c.* 1783–5. It was his principal work in the genre and shows not only the understanding with which he could paint children but a sense of the realities of peasant life

Zoffany (1733–1810) practised the genre with consummate skill, both in its more intimate form, as in the painting of Queen Charlotte in her boudoir with her two small sons attired in fancy dress (*Ill. 76*), or in the *tours de force* of grouping presented by his *Life School at the Royal Academy* (*Ill. 77*)

76 Johann Zoffany, who first made his name by small theatrical portraits, brought the art of the conversation piece to a degree of great elaboration on a small scale. This painting of *c.* 1766, *Queen Charlotte and her two elder Sons* in fancy dress, enabled him to add to the intimacy of the genre a wealth of ornate detail

and his *Cognoscenti in the Tribuna of the Uffizi* (*Ill. 78*). As a special form of the conversation piece, the portrait of an actor or of actors on the stage, such as Hogarth had presented in his scene from *The Beggar's Opera* and his portrait of Garrick as Richard III, was continued also by Zoffany and by such

specialists as George Clint (1770–1854) and Samuel de Wilde (1748–1832); many lively scenes of stage comedy by them are preserved in the Garrick Club (*Ill. 79*).

There is a Scottish equivalent to the art of Reynolds in that of Sir Henry Raeburn (1756–1823), who depicts such a gallery of celebrities in Edinburgh, in a great period of the Scottish capital, as did Reynolds in London. In the use of broad divisions of light and shade characteristic of the century he emphasizes dramatic effect and is especially well able to convey the strength of male features. His full-length figures – always an exacting test of a portrait painter's ability – indicate some limitations in his resource in composition, offset, however, by a dramatic vigour of pose and lighting. His range of colour was not wide or subtle in its suggestion, but there is a candour and decision in his work which always commands respect (*Ill. 80*).

The account of portraiture would be incomplete without some reference to the revival of the miniature in which

77, 78 In the remarkable paintings (*opposite*) the scope of the conversation piece is extended beyond its established limits to become a detailed historical document. In the *Life School at the Royal Academy* (1772) (*above*) Zoffany portrays himself, left, with palette, Benjamin West, Hayman with hands on knees, Reynolds with ear-trumpet, Zuccarelli posing the model, Wilson behind him and other Academicians. The other painting, *Cognoscenti in the Tribuna of the Uffizi* (1780) (*below*), groups English artists and connoisseurs round Titian's *Venus of Urbino*

79 (*right*) Subject painting in England in the form of the conversation piece and also of comic and tragic narrative had a long connexion with the stage, a reminder of which is given by Samuel de Wilde's *Mr Matthew as Sir Fretful Plagiary in 'The Critic'*, 1810

Richard Cosway (1742–1821) and Ozias Humphry (1742–1810) played a leading part. It cannot be said that they renewed the importance which it had had with Hilliard and Samuel Cooper, but something of eighteenth-century elegance appears in their dainty productions.

80 Though Raeburn lived until 1823 his work belongs in spirit to the age of Reynolds, who, as much as anyone, inspired the breadth and dignity of his style, best appreciated in the splendid collection of his works in the National Gallery of Scotland. In this *Portrait of Colonel Alastair Macdonell of Glengarry* (said to have been the original of Fergus MacIvor in Scott's *Waverley*) the vigour of effect is obtained both by the determined pose and the dramatic contrast of light and shade

81 In *Academy by Candlelight* Joseph Wright exploits the dramatic effect of artificial light in a way that also reflects his romantic feeling. It was painted in *c.* 1769. The statue is a version of the *Nymph with a Shell* in the Louvre

A portrait painter of an exceptional kind is Joseph Wright of Derby (1734–97) who received commissions from the industrial community of his native place, carrying them out with an admirable realism. Yet as Wilson was diverted from portraiture to landscape, Wright's interest was aroused in the changes produced by science and industry. It is combined in a complex way with a romanticism which led him to delight in effects of moonlight, candlelight (*Ill. 81*), or Vesuvius in eruption, but such paintings as those of an *Iron Forge* (*Ill. 82*), or the *Experiment on a Bird in an Air Pump* give colour to the description of him as 'the first professional painter to express the spirit of the Industrial Revolution'.

82 Painted in 1772, Wright's *Iron Forge* might be looked on as an imaginative forecast of the forces to be developed by the Industrial Revolution

CHAPTER EIGHT

Watercolour and the Picturesque

If one excludes the miniature, the history of English painting from Tudor to Hanoverian times is that of oil painting, but from about the middle of the eighteenth century watercolour comes into view as a medium peculiarly belonging to and expressive of the English spirit in art. Its development was bound up with travel both at home and abroad. One early pioneer in the latter respect was the Elizabethan artist, John White, who used watercolour in his pioneer records of the first colony in Virginia. England itself in the eighteenth century was still a land to be discovered either as regards its natural beauties or the architectural remains of the past. At the same time aristocratic patrons of the arts, going on the Grand Tour of Italy, sought out artists who would either accompany them or could provide pictures of the scenes *en route*.

There were obvious practical reasons why watercolour should be preferred to oil. The equipment was much easier to take on a journey. A tinted drawing, moreover, was far more suitable for an engraver to work from in the preparation of the illustrated works on topography and antiquities for which it was often the destined original. It was indeed a more convenient medium than oil for any work into which a topographical element entered, requiring direct execution on the spot. It was not exclusively a topographical instrument however and its rise was accompanied by remarkable developments of both aesthetic theory and technique.

83 One of Alexander Cozens's larger and more highly finished monochrome paintings, despite its title *Classical Landscape*, this is not 'classical' in the conventional sense but the imaginative completion of the suggestions provided by more or less haphazard blots and tones of watercolour. The rocks, recalling those of Chinese landscape, seem to have evolved in a similar fashion from a process of contemplation. It is a landscape of the mind and not of reality

An account of watercolour may well begin with the work of Alexander Cozens, a thinker and writer on art, in the phrase of Beckford of Fonthill 'almost as full of systems as the Universe'. Alexander Cozens (*c.* 1717–86), born in Russia, was sent to study art in Italy when a young man and, as various indications in his later productions show, he was especially interested in the aspect of landscape, so much in accord with one direction of English taste, represented by the art of Salvator Rosa with its contorted trees and volcanic rocks (*Ill. 83*). Settling in England, he became a drawing master at Eton and pursued the same occupation at Bath and in London, from 1781, being Instructor in Drawing to the Young Princes. A candidate for Associateship of the Royal Academy, he was unsuccessful, probably because he painted little in oil. He was noted in his own time and has again become of note in ours for his 'New Method for assisting the Invention in the Composition of Landscape', a method applied with most impressive results in his own mainly monochrome paintings. Accidental blots and stains, he found, as Leonardo had done long before, could suggest all sorts of images. His plan was to make such blots in quick succession, though having at the same time some general idea in mind, so that chance and design operated together. In modern terms it might be said that it was a release of the unconscious; memories of things and pictures seen came to the surface, stripped of detail but strangely vivid.

The paintings in grey and brown washes so produced have a certain relation with the 'moppings' of Gainsborough and it seems very possible that there was some interchange of influence between the two artists at Bath. In the combined freedom and decision of certain brush drawings Cozens displays a surprising affinity with Chinese painting. Their energy comes from concentrating on the purely visual aspect of composition and an exercise of contemplative faculties new in any part of the Western World.

In some respects his son, John Robert Cozens (1752– c. 1797/9) continued his work, though without the same subjective and psychological element. He retained the sense of generalized composition unfettered by topographical detail, but giving his attention to real rather than imaginary scenery. He is the great exemplar of the Grand Tour watercolourist, accompanying the connoisseurs Richard Payne Knight and William Beckford on their journey through the Swiss Alps to Italy (*Ill. 84*). Using a little more colour than his father, but still sparingly, and confining himself largely to blue, blue-grey, and grey-green, he was able to convey the grandeur and poetry of mountain masses as no one had done before. For some reason it is usual to think that only oil painters can be considered

84 In this watercolour of the *Pays du Valais* John Robert Cozens combines the abstract sense of his father's work with the appreciation of an actual scene. The Grand Tour of the later eighteenth century had opened up a new prospect of the 'sublime' in the scenery of the Alps. His restricted scheme of colour contributes to the grandeur of effect

'great', yet a judge as sharply critical as Constable could later assert that Cozens was 'the greatest genius who ever touched landscape'.

In choice of subject and in a calculated simplicity of design which approaches abstraction, Francis Towne (1739–1816) may be placed next to Cozens. He worked both in Italy, Switzerland, and England, though the two years during which he was travelling abroad saw the production of his most original work. His *Source of the Arveiron* (*Ill. 85*) in its massive oppositions of light and dark and its sense of form as form is an abstract masterpiece.

85 Francis Towne's *Source of the Arveiron* of 1781 remarkably demonstrates the inspiration given to English artists by Alpine scenery. Towne had been stimulated by a visit to Italy via Switzerland in 1780–1

86 One of the first artists to appreciate the landscape beauties of England and Wales, Paul Sandby did much of his best work in the region of Windsor, where he stayed with his brother, Thomas Sandby, Deputy Ranger of Windsor Forest. This watercolour shows a characteristic appreciation of a woodland vista and tree forms

Paul Sandby (1725–1809) illustrates very delightfully the 'discovery of Britain' which was to absorb much of the water-colourists' effort. Sent as a military draughtsman to Scotland on the Survey of the Highlands after the subjugation of 1745, his eyes were opened to the then unfamiliar beauties of Scottish scenery. He was equally appreciative of the lowland river and the beauty of ancient trees such as he found in his frequent sojourns at Windsor (*Ill. 86*), and these widely separated forms of landscape indicate his extensive range. He was one of the first artist-explorers of Wales and travelled widely through England, painting in gouache and transparent watercolour views which are touched a little artificially but never unpleasingly with a formal convention of style. It is scarcely necessary to discuss the somewhat absurd title he was once given of 'father of English watercolour', but the opinion of

87 In his early paintings and drawings Turner showed himself a master of Picturesque topography, delighting to display his skill in depicting ancient buildings. His treatment of Gothic architecture in this watercolour of *Salisbury Cathedral: View from the Cloister* is a case in point. An unusual boldness and originality is already to be seen in the composition

Gainsborough may be noted that he was then 'the only man of genius to paint real views of nature in this country'.

The practice of travelling about England to depict country-seats, parks, vestiges of ancient architecture, and beauties of nature produced in time a typical watercolourist's route in which Wales and Yorkshire were principal points. No attempt can be made here to refer to the multitude of talented professionals and amateurs, attractive often but not aesthetically outstanding, who made this insular tour; yet one minor artist may be singled out as being, like Alexander Cozens, a man with a system: the Rev. William Gilpin (1724–1804), notable among those who gave shape to the idea of the Picturesque. The idea was that roughness and irregularity of form had a value preferable to that of the formal and regular in providing the maximum titillation to the eye. It reconciled the informal

117

compositions of Claude and the rugged rocks of Salvator (the 'ideal' Picturesque) with the irregularity of windmills and watermills, canal boats, and strips of scattered woodland in seventeenth-century Dutch landscape (the 'rural' Picturesque). It rationalized the practice of painting ruins, on the ground, not of their being historical but of their offering all the variety of shape and colour belonging to crumbling walls and what Gilpin described as the 'vegetable furniture' which climbed over them. The 'rural' Picturesque appearing in both oil and watercolour may be illustrated for example by Julius Caesar Ibbetson (1759–1817), a self-taught painter who like Morland cultivated the visual possibilities of the barn, the farmyard, the alehouse. At least one striking picture however, *A Phaeton in a Storm* (*Ill. 88*), a scene in Wales amid wild rocks (conforming in their irregularity to Gilpin's prescription) advances beyond the 'sublime' Picturesque towards the exultation of Romanticism.

A great artist is to be associated with this phase of English art, Thomas Rowlandson (1756–1827), even though he satirized the search for the Picturesque in the character 'Dr Syntax', which he and William Coombe evolved from Gilpin, and does not fit entirely into a single category. The greatness of Rowlandson is still imperfectly realized, partly because he worked on a small scale exclusively in pen and watercolour and no doubt also because he is often regarded merely as a caricaturist with a somewhat coarse humour. This, however, is to ignore two important considerations. First is the quality of the artist in the delicacy of his colour, the sensitiveness of his line, the variety of composition. Second, the breadth of view which enabled him to give a picture of social life in town and country, a 'Human Comedy' even more comprehensive than that of Hogarth though without its moralistic overtones. From the city squalor of *Rag Fair*, the tumult of Smithfield Market (*Ill. 89*), and the fashionable assemblies of the theatre (*Ill. 90*), the Mall and Vauxhall Gardens he travels through the countryside noting with inexhaustible verve rustic life, the

88 In some aspects the art of Ibbetson is related to the picturesqueness of George Morland, but in this painting of 1798, *A Phaeton in a Storm*, the 'pleasing irregularity' of nature takes on the more emotionally conceived character of Romanticism

animals of farm and field, the village green, the market square, the river and sea shore. The irregularities of gable and bow-window delight his eye for the Picturesque in market towns, as also the tumble-down cottage, the beached fishing boats, though always there is the stir of human movement. The Rowlandson of the delicate watercolour is to be distinguished from the Rowlandson of the caricature prints in which he is related to his satirical contemporary James Gillray. In the watercolours he is a unique and original artist (*Ill. 91*).

The development of watercolour was in the main a land-scape development, and an essential link between its earlier and later phases is to be found in the activity encouraged by Dr Thomas Monro (1759–1833), a specialist in mental disorders

89, 90, 91 Though Rowlandson confined himself exclusively in painting to drawings delicately tinted with watercolour, he showed himself an artist of astonishing range and fertility in expression, both in figure and landscape subjects. The two opposite are among his finest interpretations of London life and episode. *Smithfield Market, c.* 1816-20 (*above opposite*) is masterly alike in architecture and vivid detail; the *Box Lobby Loungers* (*below opposite*) a scene at Covent Garden, exhibited at the Royal Academy in 1786, in character and comedy. His feeling also for country and the 'rural' Picturesque is beautifully exemplified in *The Ferry* (*above*) with its enticing woodland recesses

and amateur painter, an admirer of J. R. Cozens, whom he cared for after he lost his reason, and an ardent collector of watercolours and drawings. In his house in the Adelphi he set young artists to work on the completion or adaptation of sketches by Cozens and others, a training of importance for two youths of the highest ability, Thomas Girtin and Joseph Mallord William Turner (*Ill. 87*).

The short life of Girtin (1775-1802) was singularly productive. At the age of sixteen he was already employed by one of the antiquarian enthusiasts of the time, James Moore, in finishing the latter's sketches, and accompanied him in 1794 on a journey in search of picturesque ruins and ancient monuments. At nineteen he went to Monro, copying at this time not only Cozens but drawings by Canaletto, whose dotted architectural outlines influenced his manner of drawing with a brush. It is beautifully exemplified in a celebrated late watercolour, the *Rue St Denis*, a product of his journey to France, late in 1801, whence he returned to die in London. Meanwhile, and in the brief space of five years, he had shown a brilliant progress in which he ascended far above the topographical level, introducing into his paintings a freedom of brushwork, a bold handling of space and mass which suggested a new range of possibilities in the treatment of landscape. His *View on the Wharfe (Ill. 92)* with its expanse of rolling country and winding river and its majestic wedding of land and cloud is a triumph. The restricted gamut of colour he often used, and perhaps acquired from Cozens, is extended into a new richness and simplicity in the evening view of the Thames, the *White House* of 1800, as moving in its spaciousness and quietude, its focus on the gleam of the white building, and its reflection as a Whistler nocturne (Tate Gallery).

Turner, whose admiration for Girtin is naïvely expressed in the remark that 'had he lived I should have starved' and who evidently saw the implications of Girtin's technical advance, is a giant who is to be considered presently and apart. To continue the story of watercolour without this great and exceptional figure is nevertheless to encounter surprising feats in a somewhat younger generation. John Sell Cotman (1782–1842), frustrated in various ways and too original and unlike his fellows to find esteem in his own time, produced some of the classics of English landscape. It was his achievement to comprise form within areas so simply and broadly silhoutted and planned as to convey at once decorative value and natural truth, the supreme example being that loveliest of watercolours, the *Greta Bridge, Yorkshire (Ill. 93)*. Cotman was no less

92 This watercolour, *View on the Wharfe, Farnley*, of the later years of Girtin's short life, shows him at the height of the achievements he had then attained, the relation of sky and the sweep of river and hills conveying a magnificent effect of distance

original in oils, showing a like sense of the value of simplification combined with a feeling for the richness of the oil medium in such a painting as *The Drop Gate (Ill. 94)*. Peter de Wint (1784–1849), an admirer of Girtin, shows something of the latter's breadth of vision in his watercolours of Lincolnshire country. David Cox (1783–1859) claims attention for the development of a style which he applied both to watercolours and oils, in which by broken touches he managed to convey the stir and freshness of atmosphere in a fashion which gives him a modest, proto-Impressionist rank *(Ill. 95)*. No less brilliant than Girtin and carrying the influence of English landscape to France was Richard Parkes Bonington (1802–28), an

93, 94 Cotman painted some of his most beautiful watercolours as a young man on the banks of the Greta River in Yorkshire, when staying at Rokeby Hall in 1805, his masterpiece of this time being the *Greta Bridge, Yorkshire* (*above*) with its exquisite silhouettes and rich harmonies of colour. The inequalities of his later work were a consequence of the neglect and misunderstanding of the unusual qualities of design here shown, though his originality was never entirely overwhelmed. In oil painting he made use of the decorative opposition of light and dark shapes as in his watercolours, but added a great feeling for the richness of paint substance appropriate to the medium. *The Drop Gate* of *c.* 1826 (*left*) is a masterly example of his work in oils which he took up during his stay at Norwich

artist who until recent times has never gained (outside France, where he has always been appreciated) the importance that was his due. The vivacity of his touch in watercolour, a novelty to the French known as *l'art Anglais*, caused Delacroix to remark that his works were 'in a certain sense diamonds, by which the eye is pleased and fascinated quite independently of the subject and the particular representation of nature'. Yet it is perhaps in some few oils that the spirit of his watercolours finds its best expression, in the freshness and sparkle of atmosphere, the sense of space to be found in the wonderful *Seapiece* of the Wallace Collection or in his views of the Normandy coast in which he anticipates Boudin (*Ill. 96*).

95 The work of David Cox provides a contrast with that of Cotman which brings out the individual quality of each. In place of the static virtues of design, Cox is particularly happy in the rendering of open-air atmosphere, as in this painting of *Rhyl Sands*, sometimes giving a certain anticipation of the Impressionist approach

96 Bonington painted mainly in France, and this *Scene on the Normandy Coast* (1826) near the mouth of the Somme is one of the superb oils executed in Normandy in which all the freshness and sparkle of his watercolour technique is applied in oil painting to the luminous atmosphere and the sense of space so well emphasized by the foreground figures

It was a failing of watercolour, from the facility with which it could be used and the drawing-master conventions which were widely practised, to drift into the position of a minor art in a compartment of its own, independent of and inferior to oil painting; yet the work of a selected few reveals it as a vehicle of ideas and a formative influence on landscape in the broadest sense. It introduced and fostered the practice of open-air painting, it tended by the example of its lighter key to cleanse the palette of the oil painter and made for directness and spontaneity of execution. Its lessons were not lost on France in the early years of the nineteenth century, and it was not only Constable but the English watercolourists whose work was exhibited in the famous Salon of 1824 who created in France the excitement of aesthetic discovery.

CHAPTER NINE

Insular trends in landscape

The concentration of painters on English landscape in the later years of the eighteenth century was in part enforced by the conditions of the time, the French Revolution and subsequent war which made travel either hazardous or impossible. It was not until the brief Truce of Amiens in 1801 that Girtin and Turner could make a first Channel crossing and not until after the battle of Waterloo that Bonington could study in Paris and topographers such as Samuel Prout (1783–1852) record the picturesqueness of continental towns. That this home-keeping habit (whether from choice or necessity) produced splendid results may be ascribed to the fact that the emotions of artists were deeply engaged and that indeed rural England seemed to them a 'demi-Paradise'. Their genius was the *genius loci*. To Constable it was a prime quality of Gainsborough's early landscapes to be so much identified with Suffolk that he 'could see him in every hedge and hollow tree'. The feeling of identity with a locality was in no artist stronger than in John Crome (1768–1821), great representative of the only local school England had had since the Middle Ages. It was fitting in this broad view that he should have been born and spent almost the whole of his life in one of the great medieval centres of art, Norwich, though not the slightest evidence is to be found in his work of any surviving medieval tradition.

Born in a public-house in Norwich, the son of a journeyman weaver, a doctor's errand-boy in his early years, Crome had

97 Consistently local in attachment as Crome was, he pursued principles of a universal validity, unity of design and effect of light being central aims. They are superbly achieved in the *Mousehold Heath – Boy tending Sheep* of 1818–20

an inauspicious beginning, yet he had example to inspire him. In his isolated England there were the Dutch paintings in local collections to see. For Hobbema he conceived a particular affection. There were also the English pioneers of landscape to point the road: Wilson from whom he seems to have learned the value of that simplicity which so grandly appears in his *Slate Quarries*; Morland whose view of rural life is so wonderfully simplified and intensified in the *Mousehold Heath – Boy tending Sheep* (*Ill. 97*); Gainsborough to indicate the local attractiveness of East Anglia. It is the greatness of Crome that he always favoured the general rather than the particular and in this sense his *Slate Quarries* and his *Moonlight on the Yare* (inspired by and yet so different from the seventeenth-century Dutch 'moonlights' of Aert van der Neer and others) attain a 'grand manner' which is entirely different from that conceived by Sir Joshua Reynolds.

After apprenticeship to a local sign- and coach-painter, Crome worked for a time in London in the studio of Sir William Beechey, the portrait painter, but returned to Norwich

98 Painted in *c.* 1818, presumably in the neighbourhood of Poringland, a village some miles from Norwich, this famous work recalls Crome's admiration for Dutch landscape and Hobbema in particular. In his appreciation of the massive structure of the oak tree seen against a glowing sky he is akin to the painters of Barbizon

as a drawing master, became a local celebrity and the centre of a group of painters with whom in 1803 he founded the Norwich Society of Artists, the nucleus of the 'Norwich School'. The *Slate Quarries* may have been inspired by a visit to the Lakes in 1802. Like other artists Crome visited France in a peaceful interlude but otherwise remained, 'holding his Academy', as he said, 'on the banks of the Yare'.

In the main, apart from a certain number of sea pieces and some topographical studies of ancient Norwich, the Norwich School was devoted to those pictures of the remains of forest land, gnarled oaks on the edge of patches of wood, ponds and stretches of heath, of which Crome's *Poringland Oak* (*Ill. 98*) gives the great example. There is a likeness in both subject and style to his favourite Dutch artist, Hobbema. There is something also of Théodore Rousseau in Crome, in the grave affection he devoted to his chosen theme, and, in the School as a whole, both an echo of Dutch art and an anticipation of the spirit of the Barbizon School.

The rise of the Norwich School may be signalized by the fact that in 1823 the Society of Artists had shown 4,600 pictures, the work of 323 individuals. Many of these were amateurs and a number of others were not of outstanding character yet the figures are sufficiently remarkable, and evidently there was what Sir Laurence Binyon called 'a deep unconscious bond' linking the Norwich artists in local attachment. Crome was the great pillar of strength, though Cotman (never so entirely local in spirit though settled in Yarmouth and a member of the Society) added his own brilliance. It was under his influence that Crome produced some delightful watercolours (*Ill. 99*). About a score of artists followed these two leaders. Cotman's son, Miles Edmund, John Thirtle, and Thomas Lound are among those whom Cotman inspired; among Crome's followers were George Vincent and James Stark. With others such as Joseph and Albert Stannard, Henry Ninham, Samuel David Colkett they reflect in some degree a regionalism unique in English painting.

99 Primarily an oil painter, Crome also produced some admirable watercolours, such as this *Landscape with Cottages*, being influenced in this respect by Cotman, his main associate in making Norwich the centre of an important provincial School. Crome seems to have adopted something of Cotman's manner, as in his treatment of the silhouetted pathways of the lane and the simplified oppositions of light and dark in the foliage

In the art of John Constable (1776–1837) the tendency to concentrate on the much-loved local scene and the process by which English painters had assimilated the lessons of Dutch landscape reached their marvellous peak (*Ill. 100*). Constable seems one who was born to extend the realm of landscape painting and in him the regional sense was accompanied by gifts so great and feelings so sensitive that he contributed something of immense originality and import to the art of the world. A likeness to Crome appears in his attachment to his native Suffolk and 'all that lies on the banks of the Stour', though a comparison between the two reveals a great difference of both mind and intention. Crome was not an innovator; he was content with tradition in painting as he found it. Constable's response to nature was a more conscious appreciation of its moods which in itself made for technical departure. It was not only 'the sound of water escaping from mill-dams . . . willows, old rotten planks . . .', of the waterways that gave him pleasure as memories of boyhood but the movement of nature, the sweep of cloud shadows, the transient gleams of light, 'Light-dews-breezes-bloom-and-freshness; not one of which has yet been perfected on the canvas of any painter in the world,' said Constable himself.

To perfect them something more was needed than could be represented by Crome's precept to 'keep the masses large and in good and beautiful lines'; a mode of painting that caught and held the temperament of the scene, as none had done before. To achieve this aim it was essential to discard the conventions of which landscape had acquired a large store – the celebrated 'brown tree' for instance which Sir George Beaumont considered a *sine qua non*; to have always in mind the natural truth which, however, Constable never deemed alien from poetry.

To a point, in self-education, he followed an established road, though his development was slow and much hampered by family objections to painting as a career. He studied the Dutch painters and Rembrandt's *Mill* always appealed to this

100 Constable delighted in the farm known as 'Willy Lott's house' on his father's property at East Bergholt which he painted several times. This version of *The Valley Farm*, painted in 1835, shows him in his more elaborately constructive vein, dwelling lovingly on picturesque variety of detail. It may be contrasted with the free oil sketches of the same subject in the Victoria and Albert Museum

101 In *Weymouth Bay* (1816) Constable bears out with decisive simplicity his dictum that a sky should be 'the key-note, the standard of scale and chief organ of sentiment in a landscape'. A constant student of cloud forms, he uses them here to each of these purposes

other miller's son as an 'epoch in itself'. Ruisdael was a particular delight and in describing a Ruisdael as 'true, clean and fresh and as brisk as champagne; a shower has not long passed' Constable finds the suggestion of his own art. He studied Wilson and Gainsborough, perceiving in them the revival of landscape from a 'degraded and fallen state'. He seems to have been mainly influenced by Gainsborough in his early work until he saw a number of drawings by Girtin in Sir George Beaumont's Collection which suggested a new freedom and breadth of approach – a signal instance of the influence of the watercolour school on the course of oil painting – observable in the sketches made in the Lake District in 1806.

It seems as if the gathered force of thought, study, and observation burst splendidly forth when Constable was about thirty-five. A brilliant example of the early 'sketch' is the

102 Constable's small oil sketch *Brighton Beach with Colliers*, painted in 1824, is a triumph of keen observation, truth of atmospheric colour, and directness of handling. Though how much more than a snapshot – swift calculation has decided the effective distance between the ships offshore and the distribution of accents of light and dark

Malvern Hall, Worcestershire (1809?). The first of the large paintings sent to the Academy was the *Flatford Mill* of 1817. It was in 1821 that he painted the *Hay Wain* (*Ill. 104*) (originally called *Landscape, Noon*) which when exhibited at the Salon of 1824 had so profound an effect on Delacroix as to induce him to add new touches to his *Massacres of Scio*.

Constable did not confine himself to the part of the Stour valley which is now known as 'the Constable country', though he is essentially a painter of southern England. Hampstead, the coast at Weymouth and Brighton (*Ills. 101, 102*), Salisbury where he stayed with his friend, Archdeacon Fisher, all provided him with subjects, and in each region he brings into play a unique capacity for rendering the freshness of atmosphere and the incidence of light. An analysis of his work shows three main forms. First there are the small oil 'sketches',

103 In the large preparatory study (rather than sketch) of *c.* 1821 for Constable's epoch-making work, the *Hay Wain*, there is all the force of impression which came of direct handling and concentration on the incidence of light. The broken touches of paint suggest some kinship with Impressionist technique

paintings swiftly made in the open air direct from nature. Using panels prepared with a reddish ground he was able to accentuate the vividness of green and blue laid over it while allowing the ground to play a unifying part and suggest, where it is left in view, translucence of shadow. There are, secondly, those large preparatory paintings for some finished work in which his method is nearest to that of Impressionism, broken touches of colour used with an incomparable verve animating the canvas with sparkling movement. The finished picture sometimes established a certain compromise between this vitality and the more static and traditional qualities of finish. The difference can be seen for instance in a comparison of the *Hay Wain* (*Ill. 104*) and the free study for it in the Victoria and Albert Museum (*Ill. 103*). The former sacrifices something

104 The finished painting of the *Hay Wain* gives more of an English air to the scene, no doubt because detail is more particularized and perhaps also because the first painting has been toned down to a milder level. It enables one to understand, however, even in its touch of light on distant meadows, the sensation it made when exhibited in 1824

of life, though it is full of beautiful detail on which Constable lavished all his affection for the typical East Anglian ingredients.

There comes, however, a stage when he is able to retain all the spontaneity of the sketch with a massive completeness as in *The Leaping Horse* and the *Hadleigh Castle* of 1829. Constable was essentially an oil painter, deeply engaged with the life inherent in the paint substance. His watercolours, though sometimes as impressive as the *Stonehenge* and *Old Sarum* in the Victoria and Albert Museum, were never conceived as complete works in themselves but as notes of an oil painter. He used oil paint with a decision and a singular effect of truth which sometimes recalls Manet as much as anyone – for instance in that small masterpiece the *Brighton Beach with Colliers*

(*Ill. 102*) of 1824. The same almost uncanny identification of paint and natural effect is to be seen in the sketch of *Willy Lott's House near Flatford Mill* in the Victoria and Albert Museum, where his intimate development can be so well studied (*Ill. 105*). In some later works there is a dramatic vehemence which might almost be termed Post-Impressionist, though the studious mood in which he made a minute study of an elm tree or a careful map of cloud forms shows the intensity of his nature worship.

It is one of the ironies of English painting or a symptom of its ungregarious individualism that so great an artist left little impression on his own country and that the creative prospect he opened should be left to be explored by Corot and others in France.

105 A sketch of *Willy Lott's House near Flatford Mill* for the *Hay Wain*, probably made direct from nature in *c.* 1816. The simplification of technique is noticeably different in effect from the broken and sparkling paint which gives animation and movement to the study (*Ill. 103*), though this sketch has its own distinct brilliance

CHAPTER TEN

Blake and the current of imaginative art

It is usual to consider Constable and Turner together and yet the differences are so great between the two that it is perhaps better to separate them by some account of the imaginative and romantic currents of their time with which Constable certainly had little to do. It may be said that he was romantic in the sense that Wordsworth may be so described, that is, in his belief in truth to nature. Ultimately perhaps the affection of both for landscape was an instance of a wished-for identification with nature in a period of alarming change and political revolution. It is, nevertheless, with a sense of incompatibility that one turns to such different ideas of expression as are to be found in Constable's contemporaries, Fuseli and Blake. If this seems an abrupt divergence, it can only be said that such divergencies were a result of that individualism which had begun to assert itself in the eighteenth century. Constable himself was a great independent and not one who asserted authority as the head of a School. William Blake (1757–1827) was more vehemently and strangely so.

In intransigence of opinion he may be likened to Hogarth. A middle-class Londoner, he had a similar forthright pugnacity in his iconoclastic attitude towards such masters as Rubens and Correggio, the same suspicion of conformity and rule, appearing in constant diatribes against Sir Joshua Reynolds and the precepts laid down in the *Discourses*. What is very striking also in this great age of landscape is his utter contempt for nature and what he termed the 'vegetative' or 'vegetable' universe and his belief in the imaginative product of the human mind which scorned imitation.

Blake indeed represents a revolt against all that the eighteenth century stood for, in so far as it may be looked on as an age of order, reason, and material values. In him something of that distant and long-buried past, stigmatized by the title 'Gothick' (i.e. barbarian), came again to life. A love of the religious art of the Middle Ages was fostered in him through the researches of the antiquary for whom as a youth, under the direction of the engraver James Basire, he prepared copperplate illustrations. The carved folds of the Gothic sculpture suggested to him the ideal costume of Heaven. The bearded visage of a medieval king or knight in bronze inspired his conception of a human archetype. A likeness to the medieval illuminated manuscript appears in the marginal illustrations of his books in which text and decorations were etched and hand-coloured (*Ill. 108*). His horror of realistic oil painting caused him to devise the species of tempera painting which he called 'fresco'.

A different source of his art was the work of Michelangelo and other Renaissance masters as rendered in engravings. Their influence produced emphatic distortions of the figure akin to those of the sixteenth-century Italian Mannerists. Linear design again comes into its own with Blake and is used sometimes with individual power and sometimes with naïve or mechanical effect in works which constitute an entirely personal version of the 'Grand Style'. Today the imperfections seem of less moment than the interest attaching to the expression of a complex mind.

The themes of Blake's art were ostensibly those of tradition – Biblical stories, allegory, and subjects taken from the poets, though a stubborn nonconformity and a purely personal interpretation of religion made them distinct (*Ill. 106*). Thus the great series of 'Illustrations to the Book of Job' was not in fact illustrative but his own conception of the inward battle of the soul. His aversion from the Classical World led him to

106 The individualism of English painting has its most remarkable expression in the art of Blake, the more remarkable if one contrasts the realism of the *Hay Wain* with the visionary nature of this work, *The River of Life* (*c*. 1805), as products of the same historical period. In clear bright watercolour Blake imagines the crystal stream described in the Revelation of St John, winding its way through the groves of Paradise from the throne of God which is represented by a great yellow sun. The centuries of realistic oil painting might not have existed – there is an intuitive sympathy with medieval art, though a difference in the intellectual independence of this man of noncomformist thought

141

eschew Homer and Virgil and those fables to which the Renaissance had delighted to give sensuous form. He found inspiration rather in the thought of Milton and Dante in which he discovered symbols of what he conceived as the interior conflict of good and evil in the mind.

The creatures of his visionary world were not 'a cloudy vapour or nothing' but to be realized with a 'determinate outline'. 'He who does not imagine in stronger and better lineaments and in stronger and better light than his perishing and mortal eye can see does not imagine at all.' Instinctively Blake put himself in the position of the English artist of the Middle Ages in whose work there is so little of corporeal substance and so strong a power of linear design and the clear colour which is its natural complement.

His achievement must be viewed apart from the history of oil painting – the medium he detested, or even from water-colour in which some of his most beautiful work was done. One can relate him as little to his contemporary Rowlandson as to Reynolds, while landscape was condemned by the nature of his ideas. As a painter he is in many respects imperfect but his mastery of design transcends these imperfections in a conception so magnificent as that of *Satan smiting Job* (*Ill. 107*), the allegories of life and love with their ecstatic swirls of form, the grandeur of *Elijah in the Fiery Chariot*, the pellucid splendour of the drawings inspired by Dante. With him a Romantic vista of free expression opens, a liberation of the poetic imagination long suppressed in English painting. Yet in this respect Blake, so intensely individual in thought as to appear an isolated phenomenon, was not entirely alone.

Visually, Blake absorbed influence from a variety of sources in a complex fashion just as he absorbed ideas (the effort to unravel the meaning of which has given rise to so many interpretative studies). The modest faculty of design of Thomas Stothard, with whom he became involved in unfortunate competition in the painting of Chaucer's Pilgrims contributed to his idea of beauty in woman and child. The

142

drawings of John Flaxman helped to direct him to the value of outline. It seems evident that some examples of Buddhist art which had found their way to England inspired the style of the series of 'Heroes' – the remarkable conceptions of the 'Spiritual Forms' of Nelson and Pitt. In design he is also to be linked with Henry Fuseli, who represents another facet of the awakening Romantic spirit of the late eighteenth century.

Johann Heinrich Füssli (1741–1825), known and naturalized in England under the Italian form of his name, Fuseli, made London his base of operations as a young man. Like Blake he was an admirer of Michelangelo, his admiration also

107 A painting in the gum medium which Blake called tempera, this *Satan smiting Job* of *c*. 1825 is one of his most powerful combinations of design and colour. The red of the outspread wings of Satan, the darkness and flame behind, add to an effect which is even more impressive than the corresponding design in the great engraved series of 'Illustrations to the Book of Job'

108 The idyllic beauty of Blake's illustrations to his *Songs of Innocence* of 1789 is in contrast with his later profound and mystical visions. The spirit of the design in which 'the art permeates the poetry' is close to that of the medieval manuscript painter

tending to the Mannerist emphasis and distortion. He shared Blake's contempt for 'vegetable nature' and for realistic imitation – 'Hang Nature,' was his phrase, 'she puts me out.' He was, however, neither a mystic nor a man of religious ideas, but one in whom the Romantic passion for the strange, the violent, the dream-like, the scene of fantasy or horror had been fostered by an admiration for the English poets, Shakespeare and Milton pre-eminently, but also those in whom eighteenth-century elegance was giving way to grander and more primitive conceptions, Thomson and Gray (whose Celtic *Bard* inspired a number of painters).

The importance of Shakespeare and Milton for English painting at the end of the eighteenth century was considerable. It was in part due to the Shakespeare productions of David Garrick and the combination of imaginative subject and theatrical portraiture which they offered painters, though more particularly to Alderman Boydell's scheme for a Shakespeare Gallery which gave a great impetus to imaginative painting. Fuseli had already made that notable excursion into dreamland, the *Nightmare* (*Ill. 109*) of 1782 with its oppressive feeling of terror. His choice of subjects for the Shakespeare Gallery focused on *Macbeth* and its 'moments of terror' and

144

109 Linked with Blake in friendship and imaginative aim, unlike him Fuseli was not concerned with the conflicts of good and evil, but in a Surrealist fashion with the creation of an atmosphere of dream and hallucination. The *Nightmare*, painted in 1782, remains one of the most successful attempts to convey this atmosphere pictorially

A Midsummer Night's Dream with its elemental world of fairies and elves, in depicting which Fuseli shows a highly original fancy (*Ill. 110*).

Fuseli's art is more interesting from a literary and psychological angle than as pure painting. There is perhaps a Freudian significance in one phase, when he depicts elongated, slightly sinister figures, curiously coiffured as in *The Boudoir*. His world of dreams, from a modern point of view almost 'Surrealist', is very different from Blake's spiritual world, yet there is an interesting correspondence between them in design. The pointing arms of Fuseli's *The Three Witches* give an accusing emphasis repeated in Blake's engraving in the 'Job' of the *Just Upright Man laughed to scorn*. A prostrate figure in Blake's *America* repeats the pose and conveys an atmosphere reminiscent of the *Nightmare*. Imaginative expression demanded a special form of imaginative design. The light of day never penetrates into Fuseli's pictures, his colour has little warmth, but like Blake's his painting is of value as an emanation of the mind.

Milton was even more of an influence on art than Shakespeare, his hero (as Satan may be called) representing another aspect of Romanticism, that bold defiance in which there is something at once Byronic and Napoleonic. Fuseli's own 'Milton Gallery', opened to the public in 1799 with forty large paintings by a number of artists, illustrates the effect. Blake thought that Fuseli's *Satan building the Bridge over Chaos* was to be 'ranked with the grandest efforts of imaginative art'. The defiant figure, the immensities of the supernatural stage became a theme intensively cultivated by John Martin (1789–1854). Not a great painter, though he has found a revival of favour in this century for his adventure into a world beyond nature, Martin is still astonishing in his spectacular representations of Satanic resistance, of 'vast infinitude' and tremendous catastrophe.

In Martin's follower Francis Danby (1793–1861) there still lingers the Romantic spirit, and it may be found not only in

110 Shakespeare and Milton both gave a stimulus to imaginative painting in England. In his paintings inspired by *A Midsummer Night's Dream* Fuseli was not merely illustrative but found an opportunity of giving shape to an eerie world of enchantment

111 Strange, desolate, and tremendous prospects appealed to the Romantic state of mind. In *Liensford Lake, Norway* Francis Danby depicts an actual place, but it is evident that what appealed to him was a wildness and sense of menace which could be imagined to go beyond the bounds of reality. It has something of the apocalyptic spirit of John Martin's paintings

such a Martinesque painting as the *Opening of the Sixth Seal* with a rendering of the darkened sun and vast earthquake described in the Book of Revelation but in such an eerie desolation as that presented by his *Liensford Lake, Norway* (*Ill. 111*). The mental ferment of this age of transition from the eighteenth to the nineteenth century is disconcerting in its inequalities of talent and incongruities of aim. It takes an effort to envisage Blake, Fuseli, and Constable as contemporaries. It is strange that the influence of Blake, exerted on a group of young artists, should have produced a return to nature though this is one of the most moving episodes in the history of English painting.

CHAPTER ELEVEN

The followers of Blake

The post-Napoleonic war reaction, the withdrawal from city life into the contemplation of nature is to be observed both in literature and art in the Romantic decade, 1820–30. France gives an example in the Barbizon School; in England, the short-lived 'ideal community' presided over by Samuel Palmer at Shoreham in Kent, animated by an enthusiasm to which Blake certainly gave the impetus. It was due in part to his personal example rather than his work, the example of a lofty spirit untouched by and superior to material circumstances. And yet one small phase of Blake's productions, his woodcuts for Dr Thornton's edition of Virgil's *Pastorals* with their suggestion of a Golden Age was enough to fire the spirit of Palmer and a small circle of friends and incite them to create a Golden Age of their own. The impetus lasted for seven years, from 1827 to 1833, during which time Palmer produced a number of small masterpieces of poetic landscape. The billowing cloud, the moon, the apple-blossom in a Shoreham garden (*Ill. 113*), the moss on the roof of a barn were viewed with an intensity which gave them a more than realistic significance. The paintings in monochrome, and sometimes a mixture of media, oil, watercolour, and tempera, are imbued with emotion. It is this which accounts for an effect that cannot be simply analysed in terms of form and colour and yet is inherent in them. Once this intensity of feeling was lost, as it was lost in Palmer's later work, there remained only a pleasant talent.

112 The idea of a Golden Age which led the young followers of Blake to call themselves the 'Ancients' animates this watercolour, *The Primitive City* of 1822, a unique achievement of Edward Calvert. In colour and detail it seems almost like a medieval miniature, though it has a sensuous appreciation of the human figure in which he is distinct from Blake's other disciples

113 The fervour shared by the 'Ancients' during their stay at the Kentish village of Shoreham is most intensely found in Samuel Palmer. *A Shoreham Garden*, a watercolour and gouache painted *c.* 1829, with its clusters of apple-blossom, ecstatically seen, is an outstanding instance of his ability to invest nature with the emotion with which he viewed it

Edward Calvert (1789–1883), Palmer's main associate in the group of Shoreham 'Ancients', as they called themselves out of a regard for primal simplicities of art and living, was also briefly touched by the magic of genius and though his work of the Shoreham period was confined to a few exquisite engravings and his painting is best represented by a single example, the beautiful watercolour *A Primitive City* (*Ill. 112*), these give him a place of distinction. George Richmond (1809–96) is visited by a spark of idealism. James Linnell (1792–1882), who befriended Blake and became Palmer's

father-in-law, was apart from the intimacy of the 'Ancients', though in some of his landscapes there is a hint of their pastoral feeling. It is Palmer, however, who stands out as the truly creative spirit, whose personal vision was to give an example to English painters in the twentieth century.

The period of transition from the eighteenth to the nineteenth century was not an easy one. The Romantic spirit was agitated, erratic, confused of direction, often attempting more than it could achieve. An instance is to be found in James Ward (1769–1859) who began as an animal painter in the style of Morland but under the spur of ambition was impelled to ever more grandiose conceptions. There is great dramatic power in his *Bulls Fighting* (*Ill. 114*) and in the vast gloomy landscape *Gordale Scar* of 1815, but his abilities were not of an order that could go farther. His attempt at a tremendous allegory of Waterloo was a failure which condemned him, as he bitterly remarked, to 'be a mere Morland'. It took the genius of Turner to feel all the impact of Romantic influence and yet 'ride the whirlwind and direct the storm'.

114 The Romantic spirit takes an individual form in the work of James Ward. In *Bulls Fighting* a temperamental violence is expressed not only in the actual combat but in the tortured forms of the fallen tree

CHAPTER TWELVE

The genius of Turner

It is a remarkable instance of the individualism of English painting that two contemporaries such as Constable and Turner should be so entirely distinct. We have to contrast Constable, the home-keeping artist, content ever to remain in the south of England, with Turner the widely-travelled; the strictly non-literary attitude of the one with the poetic ambitions of the other; the concentration of energy as opposed to a wide diffusion and expansion. If a certain kinship may be found between Constable and Wordsworth it is not like that which places Turner in the heart of the Romantic movement with all its impulsion towards wild nature, infinities of space, and moments of tremendous violence. It was possible for Ruskin, very perceptively, to group a whole series of Turner's paintings under the heading of 'Flood and fire and wreck and battle and pestilence' – how sharp becomes the contrast with the placidity of water meadows and the mild variations of English spring and summer to be found in the work of Constable.

Both were artists of such greatness that aesthetic preferences or grading as between them would be out of place. Each has his unique aesthetic achievement. Yet Turner may well be considered the greater in his range of mind and inquiry. He is one of those geniuses (rightly so termed) through whom all the aspirations of an age flow and are transformed into marvel, leaving us to wonder alike at the prodigious and continual energy of the process and the magnitude of result.

Joseph Mallord William Turner (1775–1851), born a year before Constable, outlived him by thirteen years and the measure of change in the world about him is indicated by the fact that he died in the year of the Great Exhibition, his life spanning four reigns. He began on conventional lines as a young topographical draughtsman in the age of the stage-coach and ended as the most unconventional of painters in the age of the railway and Victorian industry. One of the complexities of his career is that throughout he manipulated two arts with unequalled versatility, watercolour and oil, first applying himself in each to the study of past masters and then carrying them to successive new stages as his genius unfolded. As the young companion of Girtin he studied and copied the watercolours in Dr Monro's Collection. By the time he was twenty he was a master of the topographical Picturesque and in the tinted drawing style could depict the details of Gothic architecture or the irregular contours of an old cottage with much sympathy and distinction. His watercolours of Salisbury Cathedral give an admirable instance (*Ill. 87*).

It is evident that Girtin's brief and brilliant evolution led him to develop a mode of watercolour painting, as distinct from drawing, which possessed a richness and substance more akin to that of oil. Always experimental, Turner in his thirties was developing the watercolour as a complete work of the brush, using a variety of devices, different coloured grounds, washes floated over wet paper, touches of body colour, and sometimes scraping out highlights or light detail with the handle of the brush or a knife. The resultant richness of effect is evident in the watercolours he executed while staying with his patron Walter Fawkes at Farnley Hall in Yorkshire.

The later watercolours often executed for his own satisfaction show an evolution parallel with that of his oils, shedding detail and being increasingly concerned with luminous effect and recession and ethereal delicacies of lemon, rose, and blue, made the more effective as was his wont by sharp touches of red or dark grey. At the outset however Turner had rejected the role of watercolour specialist and began to exhibit in oil when he was twenty. He seems on the whole to have been less influenced by his English predecessors than to have considered in turn the best examples he could find irrespective of country, sometimes with a suggestion of deliberate rivalry but no doubt as much in the creative spirit of adapting the suggestions they gave. This accounts for the many differences of style and effort in works executed between 1800 and 1820. The *Calais Pier* of 1802–3 (*Ill. 115*), painted after his first visit to France, was a sea piece prompted by his study of Van de Velde but startling in its original power and the observation and skill which could render all the weight and movement of the sea. On the other hand he thinks of Crome (and of Holland) in the stillness and simplicity of *A Frosty Morning, Sunrise*. The

115 In *Calais Pier* Turner gives an impression of his own arrival at Calais in the 'English packet' in 1802, though the majestic and considered design is more than an impression in any fleeting sense. The advancing squall, the curve of sails and bending of masts, the gleams of light, combine with tremendous effect. Turner at the age of twenty-seven goes far beyond Van de Velde

116 The mountainous grandeur of Switzerland made a profound impression on Turner on his European journey in 1802, the memory of which is preserved in this awesome scene of precipice and chasm in *The Passage of the St Gotthard* (1804)

117 An aspect of Turner's art distinct from his paintings in Romantic mood or in emulation of European masters, is given by the series of studies made from nature along the Thames, 1805–10. Fresh and direct, they bring him more closely into relation with the aims of Constable than any other branch of his work and add to the impression of its immense variety

most famous example is the rivalry with Claude implicit in the glowing sky of his *Dido building Carthage*. The *Liber Studiorum* (1807–19) suggested by Claude's *Liber Veritatis* gives in its series of mezzotint engravings a whole repertoire of styles of landscape composition. In *Crossing the Brook* of 1815 (*Ill. 120*) he transfers the elements of classical landscape to the valley of the Tamar with a certain artificiality of result.

So full of surprises is he, however, that between 1805 and 1810, painting on the quiet reaches of the Thames between Walton and Windsor, and contrary to his usual practice, in the open air and not from sketches, he produced a series of small

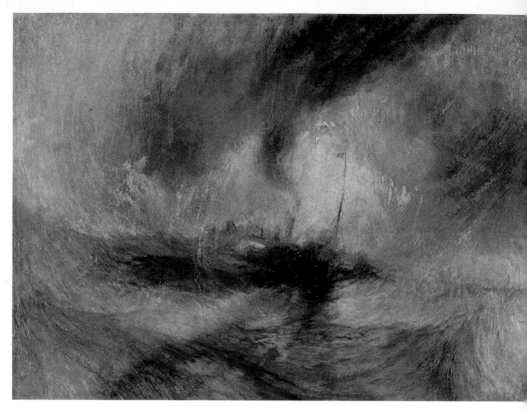

118 A work of Turner's last period, this tremendous painting, *Snowstorm: Steamboat off a harbour mouth* (1842), is quite abstract – it might indeed have been painted by some Abstract-Expressionist of modern times (if such a painter were endowed with altogether exceptional faculties)

landscapes of a cool simplicity in which he comes near to Constable (*Ill. 117*). From these he departs into the series of 'history' paintings in which some imagined scene of the past becomes the vehicle of landscape on the grand scale, providing a spectacle so tremendous as the storm of the *Hannibal crossing the Alps* (*Ill. 121*), or the fabulous Mediterranean setting of the *Ulysses deriding Polyphemus* (*Ill. 122*). There are two main influences on the outlook of the mature Turner, one being that of poetry. How far he participated in the feelings of Milton and the many landscapes described in *Paradise Lost*, of Thomson of the *Seasons*, of Byron and Scott, may be gathered from the quotations which accompanied his contributions to

119 This magnificent vision, *Fire at Sea*, painted *c*. 1834 but not exhibited in Turner's lifetime, is from one point of view a tragic representation of human helplessness in the face of elemental fury, but it is also one of Turner's most gorgeous triumphs of colour.

the Royal Academy varied by quotations from his own somewhat incoherent epic, *The Fallacies of Hope*. Without the Romantic background of poetry he would not so well have appreciated the falls of the Reichenbach, the unleashed violence of an avalanche in the Alps, the dreaming grandeur of the castles of the Rhine, the splendour of mountains (*Ill. 116*).

The other influence was that of light. The dusky atmosphere of the Thames in London may well have been the source of the 'Turner sunset' and yet it was in Italy, which he first visited in 1819, that he encountered the full splendour of light which he was to transform into the glowing visions of later years, visions in which sky, sea, and water became a luminous

120 In *Crossing the Brook* of 1815 the extent of Turner's study of past masterpieces of European landscape can be appreciated. A view in Devonshire looking down the valley of the Tamar towards Plymouth, it conforms in many respects to the style of classical landscape developed by Claude. Its aerial perspective commands wonder, though the elegant conventions of composition are not altogether expressive of the English character of the scene. It is a superb exercise in a foreign idiom

entity, as at Venice which he surrounded with such gorgeous vapour in the works he produced when over sixty years of age. The later paintings, in which he advanced far beyond the understanding of his contemporaries, are grandly elemental in their expression of dynamic force and movement on the one hand and on the other calm infinities of space. They may be aptly compared in the *Snowstorm* (*Ill. 118*) and the *Yacht approaching the Coast* of 1842. Colour gains an abstract life in the oppositions of fire and water to be found in such amazing combinations of drama and abstraction as the *Fire at Sea* (*Ill. 119*) and the *Burning of the Houses of Parliament*. It is a sheer riot of abstract splendour in the *Interior at Petworth* (*Ill. 123*).

These and a prodigious number of works beside, many of them recent discoveries from the great bequest he made to the nation, constitute an evolution for which there is no parallel. It is only incidentally that the art of Turner is related to Impressionism as it was later evolved in France. Hazlitt spoke of Turner's 'quackery' in using yellow and blue to make a visual equivalent of the green of foliage but such a quasi-Impressionist device is by no means typical. Turner's later

121, 122 Exhibited at the Royal Academy in 1812, *Snowstorm: Hannibal and his Army crossing the Alps* (*above*) shows all that sense of the immensity and violence of nature in which Turner was a true Romantic. The splendour of colour in *Ulysses deriding Polyphemus* of *c.* 1829 (*below*) has always caused it to be regarded as one of the greatest products of English art

123 The interiors Turner painted at Petworth, where he stayed with his friend the Earl of Egremont in the 1830s, are aptly described as 'colour poems'. They include this unfinished *Interior at Petworth* of 1837, with its foam of white, gold, and vermilion

work may be compared in some respects with that of Monet in the sense of atmosphere and absence of outline, but he was more comprehensive in his view of nature and at the same time more subjective. If anything, Turner seems to anticipate a Post-Impressionist development of free and abstract expression which has directed especial attention in recent times to the 'private' aspect of his work, those paintings, that is, in which he was most free and experimental as distinct from those intended for exhibition or as originals for the many engravings which recorded and incited foreign travel. The perspective of time has by now made it possible to appreciate Turner's giant stature which in his own day only Ruskin attempted to measure.

CHAPTER THIRTEEN

The early nineteenth century—age of transition

The transition from the eighteenth to the nineteenth century in English painting is strangely complicated by different ambitions and the frustration which for one reason or another hindered the career of a number of individuals. The Grand Style prescribed by Sir Joshua Reynolds, the classic perfection of figure composition, loftily removed from everyday life, never took root. Benjamin West (1738–1820) gives an example of the dullness and falsity of painting such subjects as, for instance, *Cleombrotus ordered into Banishment by Leonidas II, King of Sparta*. Not 'history painting' but historical painting was more in accord with the Anglo-Saxon temperament and the difference between the two is illustrated in West's own work. His *Death of Wolfe* was a step towards realism, the rendering of a contemporary scene in the dress of the time. His protégé in England, John Singleton Copley (1737–1815) showed a like tendency, more dramatically, in *The Death of Major Pierson* (*Ill. 124*), a work of exceptional vigour. In both painters a

124 John Singleton Copley in *The Death of Major Pierson* shows a Romantic realism which seems ahead of his time. It was painted in 1783

Romantic was concealed, appearing in that unusual late work by Benjamin West *Death on the Pale Horse* with its strangely moving confusion. Copley indeed seems to anticipate the emotional intensity of Géricault in his *A Youth rescued from a Shark*, while in the verve and movement of the *Major Pierson* there is already a hint of Delacroix's *Liberty at the Barricades*.

The deliberate attempt of others to emulate the great productions of another age and race seems to reflect a somewhat pathological aspect of the Romantic psychology, a frenzy of ambition. It is encountered in James Barry (1741–1806) with his overweening desire to excel on a vast scale and that strange confusion of heroic, symbolic, and national elements which is to be found in his wall paintings for the Royal Society of Arts, the *Progress of Human Culture*. The principal instance of this desperate and even paranoiac desire for greatness is Benjamin Robert Haydon (1786–1846), in spirit the least classical of artists despite his worship of the Elgin Marbles and the serene union of form and content they represented. In the vast scale, the passionate exaggeration verging on the grotesque, the smoky light and shade of his endeavours to achieve 'high art' there was all the imperfection of Romanticism. The real nature of his talents, against which he struggled so hard, is to be seen in the two genre paintings, now in the Tate Gallery, *Punch or May Day* (*Ill. 125*) and *Chairing the Member*, ably and unpretentiously painted and humorously observant.

Artists tended to lose their moorings in a period of unprecedented change. Deprived of the spiritual guidance which Blake had given the 'Ancients' of Shoreham they seem to wander lost in an alien world – it is surprising to recall that Samuel Palmer worked on after the brief ecstatic period of *c.* 1830 in increasing doubt and dejection until 1881, that Edward Calvert pursued some will-o'-the-wisp of Greek perfection until 1883. It is impossible to think of either as hailing the 'age of steam' with approval. It is on the contrary

125 Benjamin Robert Haydon, the personification of Romantic ambition and Romantic despair, had one of his few successes with this painting of London life, *Punch or May Day* (1829), completely different in style and character from his vast and gloomy 'history pictures' but a delightful example of genre

a sign of Turner's huge ability to take everything in his stride that he could paint a blast-furnace at Dudley, one of the new steamships in harbour, and in 1844 in his old age make a masterpiece out of the spectacle of a railway train rushing through the countryside, a spectacle at which his admirer John Ruskin could only groan in horror.

Portraiture and genre painting as practised by Sir Thomas Lawrence and Sir David Wilkie respectively are the most conspicuous features of early-nineteenth-century painting.

126 The sparkling and temperamental style in which the portraiture of Lawrence is distinct from the eighteenth-century tradition is seen to great advantage in the *Head of Princess Lieven*, painted some time between 1812 and 1820

Lawrence (1769–1830), a child prodigy to begin with and later a portrait painter of international reputation, may be considered from one point of view as the last of an illustrious line, the foredestined successor to Sir Joshua Reynolds (whom he followed as Painter in Ordinary to the King in 1792). He had a similar feeling for the charm of childhood and youth, as in the exquisite *Head of Princess Lieven* (*Ill. 126*) in the Tate Gallery; he could invest the great with appropriate majesty and distinction, though technically he introduced something new, a restless sparkle of colour and lighting, a flamboyance which is seen to great advantage in the portraits of princes and prelates, statesmen and warriors who shared in the triumph

127 The transition in the art of David Wilkie from the humour and sentiment of his early subjects inspired by Flemish genre to more serious themes and a broader style of painting is notable in *Peep o'day Boy's Cabin* of *c.* 1836. He aims for a depth of shadow recalling Rembrandt, and an expressiveness of gesture prompted by a wider acquaintance with the work of European masters

over Napoleon, the series assembled in the Waterloo Chamber at Windsor Castle.

He is now often criticized for a theatricality and a facility which tended to become merely superficial and for this there is some reason, though Lawrence provides still another interesting aspect of the workings of the Romantic spirit. His theatricality and fitful brilliance were symptoms of it; so too was that ambition to excel in the grand manner which inspired his contribution to Fuseli's 'Milton Gallery' in 1797, his *Satan addressing the Legions*, one of the resounding Romantic failures. Yet there was something of new individual expression in the sparkle of his style which engaged the attention of Delacroix, a quality analogous perhaps to that he discovered in Bonington.

It would seem that in returning to the painting of peasant and village life English art renounced the pretensions which so often had disastrous effects and gained the old security offered by the painting of the Netherlands, the example of a healthy and unpretentious realism. Engravings after Teniers and Ostade set David Wilkie (1785–1841) on the road to those minutely executed studies of character and incident, humorous and pathetic, which gave him immense popularity. *Blind Man's Buff*, *The Penny Wedding*, *The Blind Fiddler*, and *Distraining for Rent* set a style of anecdotal painting which heralded and stimulated that of Victorian popular art. What until recent times has been less appreciated is the effort Wilkie made after 1825, when he visited Italy and Spain, to develop his art along more serious and ambitious lines, though too great a facility and too little a capacity to take in the lessons of Italian and Spanish masters still leave the paintings he produced an imperfect realization of ideas (*Ill. 127*).

In this period of conflicting directions and the breaking-up of eighteenth-century tradition William Etty (1787–1849) is another minor master who attempts the romanticized version of the 'grand manner', in a style which in its glitter bears some traces of his pupilage with Sir Thomas Lawrence, though an enthusiasm for Rubens and Titian was a main motive force. His subject pictures tend to fall between the stools of insipid charm and exaggerated violence. Yet he retains a more certain place in English painting by the studies of the nude which he constantly made throughout his career (*Ill. 128*); in them a richness of colour and substance appear which no contemporary equalled.

128 Though William Etty painted 'history pictures', allegorical subjects, portraits, and some landscapes, his reputation rests on the studies of individual nude figures which he continued to make in the Life Class of the Royal Academy throughout his career. He added to a mastery of form an exceptional richness of colour in which he profited by the study of Rubens and the great Venetians, exemplified in this *Nude* of 1825

Lawrence, Wilkie, and Etty are all named by Delacroix and Géricault as Englishmen whose work greatly interested or impressed them. The 'touching expressions' in Wilkie's painting seemed to Géricault a welcome departure from classic formality and Delacroix's own historical subjects enable one to appreciate his admiration for Wilkie's oil sketch of *The Preaching of Knox before the Lords of the Congregation*. Their influence in England, however, was not favourable. In their several ways they tended to encourage an art facile and superficial both in style and ideas. Lawrence and Etty help to create the waxen ideal of Early Victorian beauty, Wilkie's early work a certain triviality of sentiment.

Sir Edwin Landseer (1802–73) is one of the most remarkable products of this Romantic phase of English painting, brilliantly and precociously gifted but long known only by those pictures which transferred humorous sentiment from the human to the animal world and departed, as Ruskin observed, 'from the true nature of the animal for the sake of a pretty thought or a pleasant jest'. Immensely popular as he was in Victorian England for works such as *Dignity and Impudence* which gave human expression to dogs, the subsequent decline of his reputation seemed absolute and final until an exhibition at the Royal Academy in 1961 gave an opportunity of surveying his productions as a whole. It then became possible to see the Scottish landscapes of his youth, when he stayed with Sir Walter Scott at Abbotsford and responded romantically to the grandeur of mountain scenery, as in *A Lake Scene, effect of Storm* (*Ill. 129*); sketch groups and portraits of spontaneous freshness; and animal studies free from banality. He may be judged by his earlier productions, up to about the age of forty, as an artist unequal and imperfect, but capable of unexpected flashes of brilliance.

By 1840 English painting seemed on the whole to have reached a depressed condition. Turner remained isolated in conceptions of a sublimity which only the youthful John Ruskin could in some measure appreciate. Watercolour con-

129 The transition from the Romantic to the Victorian era in English painting produced divergencies of effort which have made the work of some artists difficult to see and appraise as a whole. Thus Landseer has long been regarded as the essentially Victorian painter of a humorous animal genre and this has caused much of his best work which was pre-Victorian and Romantic in character to be overlooked. How good it could be appears in this Highland landscape, *A Lake Scene, effect of Storm*, painted *c.* 1836, in which his brilliant abilities are concentrated on an effect of natural grandeur, undisturbed by trivialities of detail or incident

tinued on its serene course at a level something less than great. It may be noted that Samuel Prout still continued the tradition of the Picturesque and that he and Thomas Shotter Boys (1803–72) are among a number of artists who have the modest merit of preserving for us the aspect of continental cities which no foreign topographer recorded. The marine art

130 Ruskin exaggerated when he said that 'one work of Stanfield's alone presents us with as much concentrated knowledge of sea and sky as diluted would have lasted any one of the old masters his life', but a painting such as *Off the Dogger Bank* of 1846 is the work of one who knew and loved the sea, characteristic of this prolific artist who exhibited 132 pictures in the course of thirty-nine years, his subjects ranging from Venice to the North Sea

(*Ill. 130*) of Clarkson Stanfield (1793–1867) has a very English attraction in its feeling for the chop of waves and breezy atmosphere of an estuary, though there was nothing he did agreeably which Turner did not do with more consummate power and aesthetic meaning.

There are strange pockets of decaying Romanticism as in Theodor von Holst (1810–44), a pupil of Fuseli, in whom a weird imagination can be divined, though little work remains by which to test Rossetti's estimate of him as a great artist, and Richard Dadd (1817–87) who in this gloomy decade, when Haydon committed suicide, shot his father and was thereafter confined in Bethlehem Hospital and Broadmoor. He produced some works which have a psychological interest for the present day, adding to a fancy sometimes reminiscent of Fuseli a precision of detail that heightens its tension. In David Scott (1806–49) another sombrely imaginative spirit appears whose work shows some trace of the influence of Blake.

The State patronage which took the form of a scheme to decorate the Houses of Parliament with frescoes, an effort extending over twenty years from 1841 to 1861, when the Prince Consort, its main promoter died, was disappointing from the outset. Failure in the competition depressed such sensitive entrants as Haydon and David Scott, while those chosen were hardly less put out by long delays and the technical difficulties presented in the entire absence of any tradition of fresco painting. Of all media this required most experience. Experiment with waterglass was doomed to failure; no method was known of resisting the corrosive chemical-laden air of nineteenth-century London. Nor in addition were painters trained or suited by temperament to work on a large scale in an appropriately mural style though Daniel Maclise in his *Death of Nelson* made an heroic effort.

To the gloom of art in the 1840s, an atmosphere recorded in *The Richmond Papers* and the *Memoirs* of William Bell Scott must be added: industrial depression and the agitation for political reform which found vent in the Chartist movement.

173

It was in this atmosphere that one of the most remarkable phases of English art came into being, the Pre-Raphaelite movement. Begun in 1848 as the Pre-Raphaelite Brotherhood by a group of young artists affected by the general unrest of the time, it quickly became a vital and influential force.

CHAPTER FOURTEEN

Pre-Raphaelitism and Victorian painting

Inspired like the Chartists by the spirit of revolt, the Pre-Raphaelite Brotherhood was a militant group, the first organized revolt against the Royal Academy, the objects of its attack being on the one hand the dark and pretentious history picture and on the other trivial anecdotes, and in particular what the Brotherhood termed the 'monkeyana' of Landseer. The remedy and the ideal was seen in a double aspect; as the 'truth to nature', expounded in *Modern Painters* by Ruskin and as a return to the purity of art before the High Renaissance period, along the lines suggested by the earlier 'Pre-Raphaelite' movement of the German 'Nazarenes'. There were many possibilities of complication in this duality which were to appear the more complex because of the very different temperaments of the leaders of the movement, Dante Gabriel Rossetti (1828–82), William Holman Hunt (1827–1910), and John Everett Millais (1829–96). 'Truth to nature', a conception which Constable (much more specifically than Turner) had applied to landscape painting, suggested such realism as might be gained in painting from nature, that is, in the open air, and indeed for a while this was a Pre-Raphaelite practice, showing in theory a certain correspondence with the aims of Realism and later of Impressionism in France. Yet whereas French painters were mainly concerned with the general truth of light and atmospheric effect, the Pre-Raphaelites looked for it in minuteness and precision of detail. They differed also in devoting themselves to figure subjects in the main, with an

131 One of the most beautiful of Millais's early works, *The Return of the Dove to the Ark*, painted in 1851, is moving by virtue of the simplicity in which it seems influenced by Rossetti's early oil paintings, and the emotional intensity of colour. Its quality singled it out for attention at the Paris International Exhibition of 1855

ethical and narrative content. A further difference was the tendency encouraged by Rossetti in particular to look back sentimentally and nostalgically to the past, which took on a dream-like attraction. Thus, instead of that beautifully logical development which produced the masterpieces of nineteenth-century French art, England produced a strange, though potent mixture of enthusiasms in which painting took on several aspects and eventually became subordinated to aims of wider social import.

The great period of Pre-Raphaelite painting can be placed within the decade 1850 to 1860. It is marked by intensity of feeling, a brilliance of colour which banished brown and earth

132 Painted in 1851, *The Hireling Shepherd* by Holman Hunt is remarkable not only for the minuteness of its detail but for the application of the Pre-Raphaelite aim of 'truth to nature' and the open-air effect of sunlight. The distant landscape is a reminder of the fact that in realism the Pre-Raphaelites for a short while have a point of contact with the somewhat later growth of Impressionism in France

colours from the palette (as the Impressionists were to do), and *tours de force* of detailed execution. Millais as a young man produced a number of works of great beauty with religious and Shakespearean themes. In colour and feeling *The Return of the Dove to the Ark*, 1851 (*Ill. 131*), excels even the celebrated *Christ in the House of His Parents*. His *Ophelia*, 1852 (*Ill. 133*), with its almost photographically minute background painted on the Ewell River near Kingston-on-Thames and its figure portraying the beauty of Miss Siddal, remains a remarkable picture.

Holman Hunt painted a masterpiece of its kind in *The Hireling Shepherd* of 1851 (*Ill. 132*) with a sunlit background of

133 The background of this famous picture of 1852, painted in the open air on the Ewell River near Kingston-on-Thames, is a *tour de force* of detail, while truth of effect is separately sought in Millais's study of Miss Siddal posed with floating robes in a bath. A certain photographic quality does not detract from the intensity of the total impression

willows and cornfield which for a moment makes one think of Claude Monet. The fanatic search for 'truth' which sent him to the shores of the Red Sea to paint a religiously symbolic subject invests *The Scapegoat* of 1854 (*Ill. 134*) with a Surrealist strangeness. Rossetti, apart in his poetic medievalism, reached the highest point of his art in watercolours of an imaginary past and great emotional intensity such as *The Tune of the Seven Towers* of 1857 (*Ill. 135*).

With all its curiosities of effort, this Pre-Raphaelite period has never lost its enchantment. How young artists in the industrial and mercantile England of the mid nineteenth century responded and rallied to an ideal exacting devoted toil is evident in the immediate spread of its enthusiasm and methods, though they had their effect also on artists somewhat

134 An aim at once religious and realistic found its most remarkable Pre-Raphaelite expression in *The Scapegoat* of 1854 for which Holman Hunt repaired to the Dead Sea, depicting the scapegoat with scarlet fillet, symbol of iniquity, on its salt shores. The distant mountains harshly lit, the skeletons in the water, the more-than-natural clarity of detail create an effect of strangeness which might be compared with that of some product of twentieth-century Surrealism

older than the young champions of the Brotherhood. William Dyce (1806–64) seems to reflect the quasi-photographic aspect of its realism in the enduring charm of *Pegwell Bay, Kent* (*Ill. 137*) painted probably in 1859, a picture in which he strikingly departs from a rigid style due to German Nazarene influence. Ford Madox Brown (1821–93), at first outside the movement, so far entered into its spirit as to produce some of its most characteristic paintings, among them *Work* (*Ill. 136*), with its glorification of manual labour and its brilliant glimpse of Heath Street, Hampstead. Inclined to overlabour his subject, Madox Brown displays Pre-Raphaelite colour at its best in landscapes of more simple intention.

There is an astonishing list of beautiful works by artists touched (for a brief moment in some instances) by Pre-

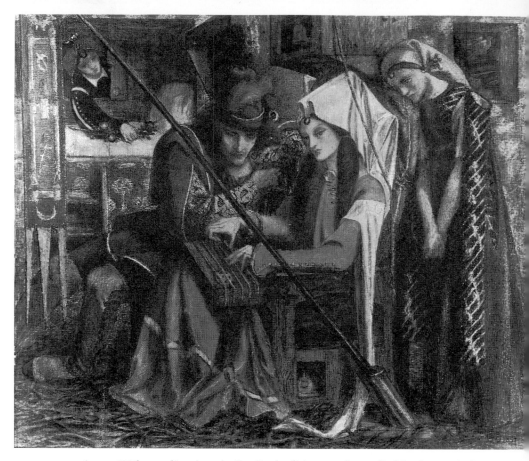

135, 136, 137 Different directions in Pre-Raphaelitism can be studied in these paintings. The watercolour by Rossetti, *The Tune of the Seven Towers* (1857) (*above*), contains all that feeling for an imagined medieval past in which his ideas and influence ran counter to realistic aims, having much effect on the work of William Morris and Burne-Jones. Implicit in Madox Brown's work painted in the early 1860s is the social conscience of Pre-Raphaelitism which Ruskin helped to foster. It represents the dignity of manual labour with a sidelong comment on the idle rich and social ills. The portrayal of Frederick Denison Maurice, with Carlyle to the right, refers to Maurice's foundation, the Working Men's College where Ruskin and his Pre-Raphaelites taught 'mechanics' to draw. *Work* (*above opposite*) is thus more than a scene on a summer day in Hampstead, though considered as such it has many brilliant passages. The landscape, *Pegwell Bay, Kent* (*below opposite*) by Dyce, first exhibited in 1860, shows the effect of the movement on an older artist and perhaps indicates some desire to emulate photography, though it has a poetry of mood which places it among the most memorable Pre-Raphaelite-inspired works

138, 139 The inspiration given by Pre-Raphaelitism to artists other than members of the original Brotherhood is here variously seen. The great promise of the short-lived Walter Deverell can be appreciated in his painting of a girl feeding a bird, in *The Pet* (*right*) of 1852–3, with its sunlit background. John Brett's *Val d'Aosta* (*left*) of 1858 carries the idea of minute representation to an extreme point and is astonishing from that point of view, though, as Ruskin remarked, it had the 'strange fault considering the school to which it belongs' of being emotionless

Raphaelite feeling, *The Pet* (*Ill. 139*) by the short-lived Walter Howell Deverell (1827–54), the incredibly detailed *Stonebreaker* and *Val d'Aosta* (*Ill. 138*) of John Brett (1830–1902), the *April Love* (*Ill. 141*) of Arthur Hughes (1827–54), the *Death of Chatterton* (*Ill. 140*) by Henry Wallis (1830–1916), the *Wounded Cavalier*, 1856, by William Shakespeare Burton (1824–1916), the *Ben Eay, Ross-shire* by John William Inchbold (1830–88), the *Naboth's Vineyard*, 1856 (*Ill. 143*), of James Smetham (1821–99).

140, 141 Henry Wallis painted few pictures in the Pre-Raphaelite manner, but his *Death of Chatterton* (*above*) of 1856 has always had a high place in the work of the School by reason of its beauty of colour and treatment of detail, quite apart from the story it tells. There is a characteristic symbolism in the guttered candle and the plant on the window-sill shedding its last leaves. Hughes's *April Love* (*right*) of 1856 was exhibited at the Royal Academy in the same year as Wallis's work, and it is possible to agree with Ruskin that it is 'exquisite in every way'. Colour again has that emotional value in itself which is so marked in the best Pre-Raphaelite works

142 *Life in the Harem* (1850) by John Frederick Lewis represents that phase of Romanticism which turned the attention of French and English artists in the 1840s towards the 'Orient'. His stay in Cairo, whence he returned to England in 1851, inspired many subjects of this kind, executed with a minuteness and vividness of colour which has been compared with that of the Pre-Raphaelites. He is, however, much more typically Victorian than they, and his work Eastern only in setting and accessories

143 Much influenced by Rossetti and the latter's interest in William Blake, James Smetham's work as in this instance was the product of religious and mystical thought which gives it an unusual intensity. *Naboth's Vineyard* was painted in 1856, the year of many Pre-Raphaelite masterpieces

It is a sad aspect of the Pre-Raphaelite story that none of these painters lived up to their first promise and in various ways lost direction. The remark applies almost equally to Millais, Rossetti, and Hunt though the decline or deflection in each case was individual. The nostalgic element overcame the challenging realism, in painting at all events. A second phase inspired by Rossetti and represented by William Morris (1834–96) and Edward Burne-Jones (1833–98) is mainly of note for a change of direction towards the crafts and the problem of providing a counter to the ugliness and soullessness of industrial production (*Ills. 144, 145*). The delicate mannered painting of Burne-Jones is of less value than his collaboration with Morris in the arts of design. In this and

144 The only purely pictorial work by William Morris, *La Belle Iseult*, an early painting (1858), indicates that he would have been distinguished in this branch of art if he had not diverted his abilities to decorative design. The subject and feeling reveal that devotion to an imagined past as derived from the *Morte d'Arthur* which colours every aspect of his expression as poet, designer, and Social idealist

other ways Pre-Raphaelitism may be looked on as anti-Victorian, a protest against the materialism of the age, either as an attempt at reform or an escape into the past, its weakness appearing in the latter respect.

In contrast is a style of painting which was essentially Victorian, uncritically reflecting the life and interests of the age and with a value in this respect which becomes more evident in the perspective of the present day and with the subsiding of a prejudice long shown towards its most typical

186

145 The art of Burne-Jones represents that last stage of Pre-Raphaelitism in which it had lost all its early militance and intensity and turned to nostalgic refinement. The personal quality of his work and his ability in decorative composition are seen to advantage in *The Magic Circle* of *c.* 1880

productions. In love of detail it has a period link with Pre-Raphaelitism though distinct from it in the absence of poetic or romantic aspirations. Remarkable in detail and typically Victorian in style though exotic in subject-matter is John Frederick Lewis (1805–76). His *Life in the Harem* (*Ill. 142*), his effects of light colourfully filtering into Islamic interiors have the minuteness of a Pre-Raphaelite, though the inmates of his harem have that insular and Victorian style of beauty which derived from Sir Thomas Lawrence.

146, 147 As well as being a master of graphic art, Charles Keene had all the qualities of a painter, as may be gauged from this rare excursion into oils in his *Self-Portrait* of *c.* 1860 (*opposite*). The realism of Victorian painting has its most remarkable expression in the work of Frith. The panorama of Victorian life of *Derby Day* (*above*), painted in 1856–8, is a complex composition, the result of numerous careful studies, both drawings and oil sketches. Apart from its burden of sociological content, it is carried out with fluent skill

More typical however is the concern with social life at home represented by William Powell Frith (1819–1909). It is the merit of Frith that after a period in which he painted illustrations to novels and costume pieces in the manner of C. R. Leslie and others, and of as little value, he became a portrayer of contemporary life, a sort of Victorian Hogarth. His reputation rests on the three comprehensive panoramas of the *Ramsgate Sands* of 1851, *Derby Day*, 1856–8 (*Ill. 147*), and *The Railway Station*, 1862 (*Ill. 148*). His fault, for which he has often been derided, is that of compressing all the incident of a novel on to a canvas, yet his acuteness of observation, the technical skill which is brilliantly evident in the details of *Derby Day*, and his ability to animate a crowded scene without confusion proclaim him a painter of rare gifts.

The nearest equivalent to Frith is to be found in Robert Braithwaite Martineau (1829–69) whose *The Last Day in the*

148, 149 Frith's *The Railway Station* (*above*) of 1862, executed with all the illustrative gusto of *Derby Day*, depicts a variety of incidents at Paddington. The composition, apart from human interest, is handled in masterly fashion, the cast iron and glass of the station roof presenting a problem of perspective which Frith turns to decided account. *The Last Day in the Old Home* (*below*) is another extraordinary piece of Victorian genre, painted in 1862 and shown at the Great Exhibition of that year. The artist, Martineau, pupil of Holman Hunt, patiently applies the same elaboration of method as his master to a melodramatic subject

150 The illustrative element in Victorian art has a magnificent product in the illustration of the 1860s, to which Arthur Boyd Houghton made a distinguished contribution. That his faculty of observation was applied also with great effect to painting can be seen from *Ramsgate Sands* of 1861. The seaside holiday was a special Victorian genre of which this is a charming example

Old Home, 1862 (*Ill. 149*) is even more of a novel in paint than Frith's *Derby Day* but elaborated with a wealth of pictorial circumstance detailed with wonderful skill. It is the merit of Arthur Boyd Houghton (1836–75) to bring the life of the 1860s vividly before us as in his *Ramsgate Sands* (*Ill. 150*), that also, of George Hicks in his *Woman's Mission*. The Victorian taste for melodrama is frequently combined with an interest in detail as in the series by Augustus Egg depicting sin and punishment, the *Past and Present* of 1858 (*Ill. 151*). In the 1870s

191

151 *Past and Present*, one of the three pictures Augustus Egg painted in 1858 with the obsessional Victorian theme of sin and punishment, provides, like Martineau's *Last Day in the Old Home*, a parallel with the melodrama of the stage

the trend was more definitely towards 'social realism', in the sense of depicting the seamy side, the life of the unfortunate and outcast – as in *The Casual Ward* of 1874 by Sir Luke Fildes (1844–1927). The reflection of Victorian life and the unpretentious art with which it was depicted are justly the object of a temperate reassessment.

Another thread of art in the second half of the nineteenth century is that of a belated classical revival, looking back to Italy and Greece, sedulously avoiding contemporary life. As previous revivals in Europe had been inspired by some new discovery of ancient art so the Elgin Marbles, installed in the British Museum, exerted, a considerable time after Benjamin Robert Haydon first admired them, an influence which can be seen in the painting of Lord Leighton (1830–96), George Frederick Watts (1817–1904) (*Ill. 152*), and Albert Moore (1841–93). They sought a beauty of fold and classic drapery like that of the Parthenon sculptures, and they pictured the ideal in a classic regularity of feature. English painting had never been altogether happy in classical emulation, and there

are flaws to be found in their pursuit of perfection. Watts
infused into his allegories an uneasy didacticism; Leighton,
more intellectual than intuitively an artist, was perhaps too
academically 'perfect'; Moore seems to paint English maidens
incongruously in fancy dress (*Ill. 153*). Yet a 'period' charm is
perceptible in these undoubtedly gifted artists, and even real

152 In contrast with the documentary trend of Victorian realism was the pursuit of an
ideal beauty both in subject and treatment of which Watts gives an example, though the
aim was confused in many works by his desire to impart moral lessons. In style and
feeling his *Portrait of Ellen Terry* shows him at his best

153, 154 The classical revival of the later nineteenth century was much influenced by the Parthenon frieze, as in *A Summer's Night* of 1890 (*above*) by Albert Moore, while both he and Lord Leighton followed the ancient model in their treatment of drapery. In their search for idealistic expression they sedulously avoided any representation of contemporary modes and manners, but their dream world has the imprint of their period, and the maidens they depict have an Anglo-Grecian style of beauty. Idealistic feeling without classical suggestion of subject can be appreciated in the painting *Autumn* of 1865 (*left*) by Frederick Walker

155 Alfred Stevens is a solitary among English artists in being inspired by the High Renaissance and his *Judith*, painted *c*. 1848, reveals in its 'grand manner' the deep impression made on him by Michelangelo during his stay in Rome

grandeur in Watts's portraits. The constant study of the figure also produced some admirable examples of draughtsmanship. Archaeology and anecdote in antique guise became substitutes for classicism in the work of Edward Poynter (1836–1919) and Alma-Tadema (1836–1912). Frederick Walker (1840–75) provides another kind of incongruity in classically arranged and posed scenes of everyday life which Ruskin unkindly termed 'galvanised Elgin' (*Ill. 154*). Alfred Stevens (1817–75) in his efforts to revive the spirit of the Italian Renaissance seems an artist of power born out of his time (*Ill. 155*), though a masterly pictorial ability appears in one or two paintings, apart from the decorative schemes and sculpture which absorbed most of his effort, the portrait of Mrs Anne Collmann being a well-known example.

Travelling as they did extensively and studying the past often with an eclectic zeal, English painters had become strangely isolated from the rest of the world, content with the

156 Though Whistler's conception of a purely aesthetic beauty was in contrast with Victorian practice, he was not un-influenced by English contemporaries. There is a blend of the Japanese print and Pre-Raphaelite feeling in the *Princesse du Pays de la Porcelaine*, later called *Rose and Silver*. The portrait of Christine Spartali, daughter of the Greek Consul-General in London, painted in 1864, the picture later set the key for the famous Peacock Room in which it was designed to have a central place

patronage of the wealthy middle class with whom they appear to have been perfectly in harmony. The task remained of distinguishing the beauty of art from the interest of story and of restoring a salutary connexion with the Continent. The art of James Abbott McNeill Whistler (1834–1903) represents as complete a break with subject and story and as conscious an attention to colour harmony and abstract design as can be found before the twentieth century.

American by birth, Whistler is indeed the first of the inter-national practitioners of an abstract art, though by many associations he is attached to the English School. In its development his painting derived something from both sides of the Channel. Perhaps more important than his early friend-ship with Gustave Courbet was the general liveliness of artistic life in Paris in his student days, the discovery of the

157 The series of *Nocturnes*, of which this one of *c.* 1870 is an exquisite example, is Whistler's most distinctive contribution to art. It is a form of painting in which Whistler seems most abstract and apart from the tendencies of either French or English art, though the atmospheric effect is especially associated with the Thames at Chelsea

Japanese print, and the selectivity of design and colour which was to be his main achievement. Yet settled in London in the 1860s he was for a while in close contact with the Pre-Raphaelite circle; the influence of Rossetti can be seen in the figures of women in meditative attitudes and the garments falling in long medieval folds favoured by Pre-Raphaelitism – from the *Symphony in White* (White Girl) exhibited in the Salon des Refusés of 1863 to the *Princesse du Pays de la Porcelaine* of 1864 (*Ill. 156*). Another aspect of English influence is a later tendency to depict a 'classical' style of figure after the manner of Albert Moore. It is, however, in the beautiful series of *Nocturnes* (*Ill. 157*) and the few superb portraits devised as 'Arrangements' of colour, such as *The Artist's Mother – Arrangement in Grey and Black* (Louvre), that Whistler is unique. Though sometimes so called, he was not an Impressionist

158 In its originality of design *Hammersmith Bridge on Boat-race Day, c.* 1862, shows the intuitive ability of Walter Greaves, and though his later works were dominated by his attachment to Whistler, this personal quality remained in his many views of the Thames

either in technique or attitude to nature. He worked from memory and according to abstract principles of restricted colour harmony and formal design, not separating colours in the Impressionist fashion but preparing desired tones on the palette. Both in painting and caustic comment he gave a denial of the Victorian Age: of the Academy subject picture and its type of narrative, of a purely literary type of criticism. He replaced descriptive and dingy colour by the exquisite harmonies which 'aspired to the condition of music'.

Whistler is a solitary man of genius considered in either a French or English relation though he had one devoted follower in Walter Greaves (1846–1931). An unlettered Chelsea boat-builder, Greaves produced that extraordinary picture *Hammersmith Bridge on Boat-Race Day (Ill. 158)* when he was about sixteen, possibly before he met Whistler, displaying all the naïve brilliance of colour and sharp delineation we now associate with the art of the child and early adolescent,

ISOLDE

159 The recurrent emphasis on line in English art strikingly appears in the work of Aubrey Beardsley, mainly in black-and-white, but sometimes supported by subtle washes and touches of colour as in this work, *Isolde*. As much apart from oil painting as the art of Blake, his graphic brilliance dominated a decade

though with an unusual and maturer power. Later nocturnes of the Thames testify to Whistler's spell, though often with some sharp touch of design which makes them distinct.

The end of the nineteenth century presents a somewhat confused picture, in which only one factor is at first clear – that the Victorian Age had come to an end. One who set the stamp of *fin de siècle* on art was Aubrey Beardsley (1872–98) (*Ill. 159*), though apart from one or two essays in colour he confined himself to draughtsmanship – as that other isolated genius Charles Keene (1823–91) had done, though even a rare oil sketch serves to indicate that he was an artist who could have excelled in painting (*Ill. 146*). In various trickles the influence of French Impressionism begins to appear though the overflow of that broad and splendid channel of painting was on the whole slight or indirect. John Singer Sargent (1856–1925), American but, like Whistler, English in association, applies to portraiture, somewhat superficially but with dazzling

160, 161 Line and tone rather than colour were on the whole characteristics of English painting at the end of the nineteenth century. There is a *fin de siècle* elegance in the slender length of Sargent's *Portrait of Graham Robertson* (1895) *(left)*. A preoccupation with tone gives a special distinction to Sir William Rothenstein's *The Doll's House* (1899) *(right)*

virtuosity, a play of light effective rather in bringing more saliently into view the character of the sitter than possessing an inherent value of colour (*Ill. 160*). A sense of tone derived distantly from Whistler may be found in a number of able painters, in *The Doll's House* by Sir William Rothenstein (1872–1945) (*Ill. 161*), in the still-life of Sir William Nicholson (1872–1949) (*Ill. 163*), in the imaginative views of buildings, decrepit and strange (*Ill. 162*) by James Pryde (1866–1941), though they show the variety rather than the homogeneity of painters formed towards the end of the nineteenth century.

162 *The Slum* (1916), by James Pryde, whose Romantic imagination creates a strangely impressive world of phantoms, architectural and human. He gives some pictorial reminiscence of Edinburgh and London and his style pays its tribute to Guardi, but the result is a creation apart

Yet Impressionism found a certain focus in the New English Art Club founded in 1886, two members of which stand out, Philip Wilson Steer (1860–1943) and Walter Richard Sickert (1860–1942).

It seems to have been difficult for painters in the Late Victorian and Edwardian atmosphere to have realized the possibilities of forward movement, the vital impetus contained in French Impressionism which was not merely an ingenious device for rendering atmospheric effect but a whole new prospect of colour. In Wilson Steer, a conservatism which was perhaps the legacy of a century in which England had remained aloof and apart from the Continent, interposes at a certain point to prevent a realization of this essentially modern value. His early work, produced after a period of study in

Paris (1882–4), splendidly and fully participates in the discoveries of colour still being made in France by the 'Neo-Impressionists'. A sparkling vitality and crispness of design gives the paintings executed at Walberswick and Cowes in the 1890s a place of special distinction in the history of modern English painting (*Ill. 165*). For a moment he seems akin to Seurat. In the early years of this century, however, settled in England, which he never again left, he turned back for inspiration to Constable and Turner. His most characteristic works are those in which he painted the transient effects of light on English scenery, as in his *Richmond Castle* (*Ill. 164*) of 1903, though with less of the freshness and clarity of his earlier style which was now completely changed. The most original contri-

163 *Gurnards* is an example of Nicholson's mastery of tone and design in still-life painting. More realistic in effect than his graphic art, there is an unobtrusive simplification which recalls the faculty for simplified design he had shown (together with James Pryde) in woodcuts and poster design

164 In this painting of *Richmond Castle* of 1903, Wilson Steer approaches English landscape in the same spirit as Constable with emphatic brushwork and transient effects of light

bution of the later Steer to English painting is probably to be found in his revival of watercolour landscape, swiftly and directly executed in the open air. The conception of him as an artist superior, by virtue of refusal to interest himself in ideas, or the supposed eccentricity of modern painting, tends to be replaced by that of a modest and able painter whose abilities were retarded by a somewhat passive habit of mind.

From a present-day point of view Walter Sickert is a much more considerable and powerful personality, to some extent conservative also, but with an alertness of intelligence and capacity for advance which are conspicuous throughout his long career. Though he worked for a while with Whistler as a young man and acquired from him the practice of etching he can scarcely be considered his pupil. He learned much more from Degas and may be regarded as an Impressionist in the same limited sense as the French master. Like him, Sickert never painted in the open air but constructed his pictures from

165 The early paintings of Wilson Steer at Walberswick in the 1880s are brilliant creations in a vein different from that of his later work, marked by a freshness and Neo-Impressionist incisiveness of colour and feeling which can be appreciated in this example of 1895, *Girls running: Walberswick Pier*

slight sketches made on the spot, carefully squaring up the drawings for enlargement so as to retain the appearance of spontaneity. He was much more interested in people and city life and its architectural background than in landscape, and in general in the artificial lighting of an interior than in the light of day. There is an interesting correspondence between some phases of his art and those of Degas – the paintings of the music hall are equivalent to those of cabaret and café-concert, the nudes in dim and squalid rooms are as unconventionally natural as Degas's paintings of *le tub*. He never hesitated to make free use of photography as Degas had done and he is

166 The attachment to the music hall which Sickert evinced in the 1890s, as in *Old Bedford* of 1897, reflects the naturalism of the period. Like Degas, of whom he was a faithful disciple, he found a rich source of material in the showy architecture, effects of artificial light, and relation of audience and stage in the place of popular entertainment

much nearer to his freedom of style than to the abstract elegance of Whistler against which his work was a reaction. In his robust realism there was something of Hogarth as well as of France.

Viewed as a whole his work, far from appearing that of a minor follower of Impressionism, is that of an original master. The 1880s and 1890s, palmy days of the music hall, produced their richly dusky souvenirs of the *Old Bedford* (*Ill. 166*) and *Gatti's Palace of Varieties*; Dieppe, Paris, and Venice in the first decade of the present century, their memorable interpretations of architecture. In the Camden Town period of

1905–14 we see him fascinated by London's rich shabbiness; later at Bath and Brighton he tends to work in clearer, flatter colour than before but with undiminished brilliance, and always with a defiance of conventional taste. Though he regarded with scepticism the progress of French painting from Cézanne onwards he had his own evolution of style in which there is an increasing liberation of form and colour.

An unusual facility in mural painting was that of the many-sided Sir Frank Brangwyn (1867–1956). Given a bent towards decorative art by early employment with William Morris and with a liking for strong colour heightened by travel in the East, he was equipped to carry out those large-scale decorative commissions which gained him an international reputation in the Edwardian period. His decorative style is little related to the general trend of English and modern painting, but in an early twentieth-century phase of mural painting he gives in some respects an English equivalent to Diego Rivera and José Maria Sert with whom he contributed to the decoration of the Rockefeller Center, New York.

CHAPTER FIFTEEN

Varying directions of the twentieth century

Any attempt to give an ordered and logical sequence to English painting in the early twentieth century would be artificial, since there was no main current such as appeared in France at that period. A basis or standard of effort may be found in the Slade School under the direction of Henry Tonks, which inculcated a severe discipline of draughtsmanship but suggested no particular approach to painting except in the negative sense proposed by its professors that there should be no accommodation with a modern foreign art that was looked on with a deep and still Victorian suspicion. It was an attitude implied with contemptuous indifference by Wilson Steer, vehemently expressed by Tonks for whom Cézanne became a symbol of wrongdoing, indeed an arch-enemy.

From the Slade School came a succession of thoroughly-trained and able draughtsmen, but if they are linked in this respect, as painters they are in an isolated sense individuals, in a sort of interim between a world of tradition and the world of change. One of the most remarkable of these painters is Augustus John (1878–1961), an artist of natural genius and extraordinary virtuosity who stands quite alone. His many beautiful drawings of the figure go far to justify the description of him as 'the last of the old masters'. As a portrait painter he revived the splendour of tradition, though with a tempera-mental vigour of style all his own. A native feeling for the poetic and romantic led him to depict poets from Yeats to

167 Augustus John was always at his best in the portrayal of those whose personality especially interested him, men of letters notable among them. His undated portrait of *Dylan Thomas*, the Welsh poet, was probably painted *c*. 1938

Dylan Thomas (*Ill. 167*) with particular understanding and sympathy. His early landscapes with figures, products of excursions into Wales and Connemara, are idylls of simple life often showing a singular purity and brilliance of colour. A capacity for large-scale composition, never fully realized, is shown in the mural decorations for which he left magnificent proposals. He contributed nothing new to painting as a mode of expression but remains a great independent.

To be associated with John in colour and affectionate response to mountain scenery is James Dickson Innes (1887–1914) who in a short career produced small landscapes in which colour vibrates with life. Also a product of the Slade

168 One of the many studies John made of his own children, this portrait of *Robin*, the third son of his first marriage, was painted *c.* 1909. The certainty of modelling, free play of the brush, and glow of colour place it among his finest works

School, Augustus John's sister, Gwen John (1876–1939), who might almost be called the Berthe Morisot of English painting, painted exquisite single figures in quiet tones, the value of which is unimpaired by changes of style and taste (*Ill. 170*). The historian cannot leave out of account Sir William Orpen (1878–1931) who rivalled John in promise at the Slade though falling into that category of professional portrait painters whose work has the permanence of portrait record rather than that of superior quality (*Ill. 171*). In Henry Lamb (1885–1960) there is another fine Slade draughtsman and unobtrusively gifted painter whose work has a moment of inspired exaggeration in his portrait of Lytton Strachey (*Ill. 169*).

169, 170 Henry Lamb's *Lytton Strachey* of *c*. 1911 (*left*) is a remarkable example of portraiture in which every detail seems to contribute to the presentation of the sitter's character and a studied effect of languor. The exaggeration just avoids caricature, though a certain artificiality of style, interesting in itself, sets the work somewhat apart from the artist's other paintings. Restraint and subtlety of tone, characteristic of Gwen John, appear in her *Self-Portrait* of *c*. 1900 (*right*), in which she seems close to Whistler in outlook, though with a decided individuality of style

After Augustus John, English individualism has its peak in Stanley Spencer (1891–1959), another pre-1914 student of the Slade, who took that stubbornly idiosyncratic course which has so often been noted. As a religious painter and mural decorator he is like no one else, a visionary as much on his own as Blake with whom in some respects he may be compared. He was similarly a religious painter without denomination with a like capacity for incorporating incidents and characters of the present day in timeless parables. A religious painting, he said, 'is not necessarily a painting having a specific religious subject but something where you feel its presence'. It was woven into his life at his natal riverside village Cookham-on-Thames, where he could imagine, at a regatta in Edwardian days, Christ preaching from the Horse

171 *A Bloomsbury Family*, a latter-day conversation piece painted in 1907 by Orpen, showing Sir William Nicholson and his family in his house in Mecklenburgh Square. Sir William's wife, sister of James Pryde, stands against a wall covered with Dighton prints; Ben Nicholson is seen at the table on the right

Ferry barge, from which used to be given 'Grand Evening Concerts'. His *The Resurrection* (*Ill. 172*), in what is still the most impressive of the many versions he painted, finished in 1927, is set in Cookham churchyard, the artist and his wife Hilda appearing among those who rise from their tombs.

It is as a naïve visionary that Spencer has a peculiar eminence, though the clear-cut design which seems the necessary accompaniment of the mystic's thought, as in *Swan Upping*, has its own value. Believing that 'only goodness and love and Christian and other benign beliefs are capable of creative works' he attached no separate weight to execution though his sense of composition on a large decorative scale and his detail are equally intense in effect.

Spencer did not confine himself to religious subjects. His many landscapes are carried out with something of the early Pre-Raphaelite naturalism. In portraits and a number of domestic and conjugal themes his work sometimes takes on an unprepossessing hardness or, as in the *Beatitudes of Love*, a grotesque ungainliness, reminiscent of the German 'Neue Sachlichkeit'. Yet this is evidently a fortuitous likeness, for no painter could be more local in attachment or ideas. Like Augustus John he has left no impress on the art of others, but in an entirely different sphere he must be accounted one of the most creative and imaginative English painters of this century.

Other artists, however, felt a need for a resumption of the long-interrupted relation with Europe, having an intuition of the dynamic impulse which had been given to art by the work of the great Post-Impressionists in France, and the swiftly developing movements which had followed in their wake. It was, understandably, a slow process if one bears in mind the long history of isolation. England had scarcely begun to appreciate Impressionist art at a time when Cézanne and Gauguin had already refashioned it in their various ways, when Matisse had made the brilliant departures in colour of Fauvism, when the Cubists had proposed the daring invention of a new pictorial language.

Was it a necessary process? An alternative 'return to tradition' now raised the question of what tradition? If to that of the Victorian Age (assuming this were desirable) it had already disappeared or was decaying by 1910. For art to live it was necessary that it should be of its own time. It is the progress of these efforts which from a present-day point of view gives proportion and a measure of coherence to the story of English painting in the last fifty years. It may well begin with the formation of the Camden Town Group in 1911, which Walter Sickert, despite his prejudices, was instrumental in bringing together. Meetings in his studio from 1908 onwards made possible that exchange of ideas which is so often fruitful among artists. They resulted in the formation of a

172 Spencer's *The Resurrection* is one of the most remarkable of modern religious paintings in conception and execution, and was regarded by the artist as a possible altarpiece. The effect aimed at was one of serenity and happiness. The setting is Cookham churchyard with the River Thames beyond. God the Father and Christ with the little children are seen in the porch. Both white and coloured people are represented. The artist appears twice, leaning on a tomb near the porch and reclining at right. His wife Hilda is portrayed on the overgrown grave in the foreground, also at left smelling a flower and climbing a stile in the distance going towards the river (of Life). The painting, begun in 1923, was completed in 1927, but the artist returned to the theme in *The Resurrection of Soldiers, Macedonia,* 1928–9, and a related series of paintings, 1945–50

'group' in the same year as the Post-Impressionist Exhibition organized by Roger Fry at the Grafton Galleries produced its angry controversies, the abuse of public and critics, an intensified dissension among artists. It was in this unsympathetic milieu that the Camden Town made headway and its products now take on, with the perspective of time, an appreciable beauty. A provincial school, in the sense of being dependent on a centre elsewhere, it has nevertheless a quality of its own. Its title 'Camden Town' and a certain amount of its subject-matter reflect Sickert's partiality for London's mean streets, not perhaps the most obviously suitable vehicle for new exercises in colour, yet with various insular modifications, tempering the intensity of Van Gogh, the exotic richness of Gauguin, assuming a chromatic distinction. Within the shared

173 A link between English painting in the early twentieth century and the Neo-Impressionist phase in France, Lucien Pissarro was an influential member of the Camden Town Group. The modification of his early Neo-Impressionist style, applied to English landscape as in this painting of 1916, *Crockers Lane, Coldharbour*, closely relates his work to that of the English-born members of the group

174 *Mornington Crescent* of 1911 shows all Gore's ability to transform the commonplace aspect of the London scene by the freshness of his vision and mode of treatment

aim of expression through colour various personalities are distinct. Lucien Pissarro (1863–1944), the son of Camille Pissarro, settled in England and, in Sickert's words 'a guide or let us say a dictionary of theory and practice on the road we have elected to travel', represents the Late Impressionism influenced by Georges Seurat, in which a concern for structure of design is combined with a pointillist technique. It is used with a quiet and unassuming merit in such English landscapes, painted in the open air, as his *Crockers Lane, Coldharbour (Ill. 173)*. Spencer Frederick Gore (1878–1914) shows a development from the broken pointillist colour of his early work to a broader handling in which his study of Cézanne is apparent. His capacity for investing the commonplace scene with a magic of colour is to be seen in such a work as the *Mornington Crescent (Ill. 174)*. Harold Gilman (1876–1919) was

175 The Post-Impressionist combination of definite colour and firm design-structure gives distinction to this portrait of *Mrs Mounter at the Breakfast Table* of 1916, though Gilman's interest in character and the character of his charwoman sitter add an unmistakably English element

176 In urban subjects such as this *Flask Walk*, Charles Ginner showed a sense of design and of the rich effect of paint thickly applied which derived from Post-Impressionist example, though these qualities are combined with topographical purpose

177 Early acquainted with the Neo-Impressionist and Post-Impressionist art of France, in *Cabyard at Night* of 1910 Bevan uses a pointillist technique with understanding though without loss of interest in his London subject-matter

the exponent of a prismatic palette, influenced especially by the colour of Van Gogh and attaining a jewel-like glow in such a painting as the *Mrs Mounter at the Breakfast Table* (*Ill. 175*). Charles Ginner (1878–1952) applied, if with something of a formula, a Post-Impressionist solidity of structure and paint to the local subject as in his *Flask Walk* (*Ill. 176*). Robert Polhill Bevan (1865–1925) who spent two years (1893–4) at Pont Aven, Brittany where Gauguin was working, derived from that master a simplification of form and colour which was happily fused with his delight in both landscape and town views, in which the cabs and horse-carts of old London appear (*Ill. 177*), with unexpected attraction in a new synthesis – leading one to recall that in 1910 André Derain as a French visitor to London could successfully apply to views of the city all that freedom of colour characteristic of a later than Post-Impressionist art.

Not one 'seed was blown from overseas', to adapt George Moore's remark on Impressionism, but a variety, which

178 Painted in 1956 this still-life of *Flowers* retains all the decorative quality which Duncan Grant had early displayed in his designs for the Omega Workshops, 1913–19, derived to some extent from motifs in Cubist and Fauve paintings, but used with an individual fluency

settled here and there in England producing their individual and hybrid blooms, sometimes incapable of further reproduction in alien ground, or reverting to some more insular type. The art of Duncan Grant (1885–1978) in its earlier phases shows and most sensitively makes use of the freedom of colour and design suggested by the work of Matisse, of the sense of structure which the Cubists had gained from Cézanne. *The Tub* of 1912 is a delightful revel in pictorial freedom, a release from inhibitions, one of many gaily adventurous paintings. An instinct for decoration brings this period of experiment from the realm of theory into that of surface ornament. Duncan Grant transfers flat colour and linear flourish from the canvas to design in a domestic relation, in the now rare products of the Omega Workshops, started by Roger Fry in 1913. The decorative spirit never deserted him though a more objective and naturalistic style of painting, in landscape, still-life, and portraiture characterizes his painting from the 1920s onwards (*Ill. 178*). There is a parallel evolution in the work of Vanessa Bell (1880–1961) who about 1914 displays the tonic influence of Fauve colour and simplicity of design but later with more reserve and less of outward display pursues a naturalistic course (*Ill. 179*).

From the seed of Fauvism springs a more richly spectacular bloom in the art of Sir Matthew Smith (1879–1959). The original contact with the Continent set in train a development which was to continue through the years with augmenting brilliance. Key experiences were a period spent at Pont Aven, 1908–9, where the spirit of Gauguin lingered and a period in Paris, 1910–11, where he was impressed by the painting of Matisse and a brief period spent in the French master's painting school. A striving for the 'architecture' which Matisse commended to his class in the drawings of Signorelli may be found in the remarkable nude studies of 1916, and an arbitrary force of colour like that of the Fauves in the Cornish landscapes of *c.* 1920. What followed was the welding of form and colour with sumptuous effect and especially in paintings

179 The strong impression made by modern French painting as seen in London in the Post-Impressionist Exhibition of 1910–11 can be appreciated in Vanessa Bell's vivid treatment of this portrait of *Iris Tree*, 1915

of the nude (*Ill. 180*) and of flower and still-life. It is consistently present in the 'torrent of beauty' (as an admirer has well called his pictures) which gives him a unique and important place in English art.

The seeds of Cubism and Italian Futurism made for a different, an aggressive and dynamic impulse in the disturbed and actively fermenting period preceding the 1914–18 war. One could hardly find a greater contrast than that between the sensuousness of Matthew Smith's art and the metallic and intellectual quality of Percy Wyndham Lewis (1884–1957)

180 Though the source of Matthew Smith's approach to painting may be found in the Fauve art of Matisse, he developed a richness of colour and substance in which he has a more general affinity with the great European colourists, as in the sumptuous figure works of the 1920s of which this *Model Waking* is an example

who alone among English painters stands out as the leading figure of a theoretic movement – Vorticism. Leaving the Slade School in 1909, well drilled in its standards of draughtsmanship, he shared in the interest of the time in Post-Impressionism, after a time looking towards that trend in Cubist art which developed the qualities of abstract geometrical form and provided a basis for the style expressive of a machine age which the Italian Futurists demanded in fiery manifesto. A natural rebel Lewis responded to its fervour, though rebelling against Futurism itself. His publication *Blast*, appearing on the eve of war in 1914, was a manifesto in praise of machine forms and in condemnation of the softness and sentiment of English art and the English attitude towards art, worthy of Marinetti himself.

According to Lewis the aim of Vorticism in painting was to 'build up a visual language as abstract as music', for which 'the world of machinery' offered a valid source. Early compositions included forceful arrangements of sharply angular forms which forcefully illustrate his theories, though at a later date he was to repudiate the idea of abstraction. In portraiture he strikes a balance, not always successful, between likeness and a system of mechanistic shapes. His complex and ingenious mind could conceive 'a scene of the fourteenth century' translated into mechanistic terms, *The Surrender of Barcelona*, 1936 (*Ill. 181*), being a remarkable and strangely imaginative result. His immense energy divided between writing and painting has left results still difficult to assess but always bearing the stamp of an original personality.

'Vorticism,' said Lewis, 'was what I personally did and said, at a certain period' – a *boutade* which need not prevent recognition of the fact that a number of artists shared, if not the

181 The nonconformity periodically appearing in English painting has an unusual instance in the work of Wyndham Lewis, leading to both an interest in and dissatisfaction with Cubist and Futurist ideas. His independence is to be seen in this remarkable painting of 1936, *The Surrender of Barcelona*, in which he set out to paint a fourteenth-century scene in a modern manner – as he said, an effort 'a little outside the natural-non-natural categories dominating controversy today'

argumentative nicety of his ideas the desire for a dynamic principle or the interest in machine forms. C. R. W. Nevinson (1889–1946) who studied art in Paris in 1912 after a period at the Slade School was more uncritically responsive to the ideas of Marinetti than Lewis, though both had joined in welcoming the Italian poet to London in 1913. Nevinson's Cubist-Futurist paintings, a little after the style of the Italian Gino Severini, and his paintings of the 1914–18 war (*Ill. 182*) with their sense of relentless and dehumanized movement are products of this enthusiasm which have lost none of their value with the passage of time. William Roberts (1895–1980) was a member of the Vorticist Group for whom the mechanistic idea was the result of a personal study of Cubism and Futurism which led to the production, first of abstract geometrical forms and later to that kind of genre in which he seems to convert the incidents and characters of everyday life into a grotesque and mechanized ballet. David Bomberg (1890–1957),

182 Much influenced by the Futurist movement and one of those who welcomed its leader, Marinetti, to London in 1913, Nevinson applied the dynamic principles of Futurist style in their grim appropriateness to the 1914–18 war. *Star Shell* is one of the paintings in which he vividly translated experience of service in the Red Cross and RAMC between 1914 and 1917. Their energy of design raises them above the illustrative and documentary level

183, 184 Bomberg was one of the painters strongly affected by the turmoil of ideas in his student period, the years 1910–13, and by the combined impact of Cubism, Fauvism, and Futurism. The first results were abstract paintings in which he sought an art of 'pure form'. His later work, however, departed from conventional modern devices, seeking to embody feeling in the heavily modelled substance of paint. In this respect he had a delayed, but considerable, influence on painting in England since 1945. *Mudbath*, 1912–13 (*below*) and *Portrait of the Artist*, 1937 (*right*)

equally exposed to Cubist influence and associated with Vorticism to the extent of taking part in the Vorticist Exhibition of 1915, followed a different direction proceeding from geometrically abstract designs (*Ill. 184*) to paintings in which a massive impasto is powerfully and dramatically built up in such a way as to seem charged with a mysterious significance – a method in which after many years of comparative obscurity he has again influenced artists of a younger generation (*Ill. 183*). Edward Wadsworth (1889–1949), coming from the industrial West Riding of Yorkshire, was for that reason in Lewis's view the readier to share his attitude to machine forms and certainly showed this spirit in paintings which gave to man-made objects of mechanical use a formal attraction.

War imposed a moratorium on Cubist and Futurist controversy and yet could only be truthfully seen by the means these artists had devised. As Fernand Léger in France saw the *poilus* and their guns in the identification of mechanistic forms, so the English painters depicted warfare in terms of Cubism and Futurism. The 'dazzle camouflage' of ships as interpreted by Wadsworth was a Futurist design. An intense and abstract energy pervaded the pictures of machine-gunners by Roberts and Nevinson. War was a point of departure for a young artist of previously more conservative background, Paul Nash (1889–1946) (*Ill. 185*). With something of the mild poetry and landscape predilection of the watercolourist and previously apart from the ideological rough and tumble of Vorticism, he was profoundly stirred by the spectacle of devastation on the Western Front, which inevitably he was prompted to render in abstract terms that contained and expressed its tragedy.

The decade which followed, the 1920s, had less of the shock and stir of ideas than the opening years of the century. Painters were uneasily placed between two poles – on the one hand a resistance to influences from across the Channel which even at this late date caused the 'battle of Cézanne' to be fought again, with Roger Fry as a belated champion but still encountering great opposition; on the other the spectacle,

185 The art of Paul Nash passed through several phases and this picture shows him in an interim period between what may be called a romantic Cubism or Constructivism and his later imaginative development. Together with his interest in geometrical shapes there appears a poetic transposition of reality. His work never entirely lost touch with reality. This picture, *Northern Adventure*, in one aspect a fantasy, was painted in 1929 from the artist's rooms in London which looked towards St Pancras Station, the station approach and a poster-hoarding being elements of its design

brilliant but somewhat daunting from an insular point of view, of the meteoric rise of the international School of Paris with Picasso as its protean genius. More than before it seemed necessary to English painters to study and work in France, though often with a feeling that an English painter was somehow disqualified by nationality from playing any prominent part in the general forward movement.

This, at least, was a mood of the time, heightened probably by the influential criticism of Roger Fry with its assumption of an inherent and ineradicable provincialism in the English School and the further assumption (with which John Ruskin would certainly have disagreed) that to be provincial was inevitably to be second- or third-rate. Yet from a present-day point of view many works of singular merit were produced by artists whose work is not confined by arbitrary limits of

186 One of the most original of Wyndham Lewis's portraits is this of *Edith Sitwell*, carried out with a notable consistency of style and distinction of colour. It was begun in 1923 at a period when the artist's relations with the Sitwell family were close, though it was not finally completed until about 1935

date. It is a period in which Sickert with unfailing zest creates works as original as the portrait of Victor Lecour, 1924 and the *Raising of Lazarus*, 1927; Wyndham Lewis his memorable *Edith Sitwell*, 1923 (*Ill. 186*); when Matthew Smith shows an increasing gorgeousness of colour in a remarkable series of nudes; when Stanley Spencer arrives at the achievement of *The Resurrection* (*Ill. 172*) and the great wall paintings of the Memorial Chapel at Burghclere; when Paul Nash arrives at admirable accommodations between abstraction and nature as in the *Winter Sea* of 1925 and the *Wood on the Downs* of 1929. In the work of Mark Gertler (1891–1939), whose career was to be cut tragically short, there could be seen in this decade a notable effort to reconcile a personal adherence to realism with the Post-Impressionist emphasis on the definition of form and heightened colour value (*Ill. 187*). Bernard Meninsky (1891–1950) is another artist who applied the lessons of Post-Impressionism in figure paintings of scholarly distinction.

Typical of the young painter responsive to the freedoms of the School of Paris is Christopher Wood (1901–30) whose all too short period of painting activity produced Breton and Cornish coastal scenes which have stood the test of years and have an individual rather than a borrowed *naïveté* of style (*Ill. 188*). Of more import, however, is the art of Ben Nicholson (1895–1982) who was to emerge after a long period of consistent

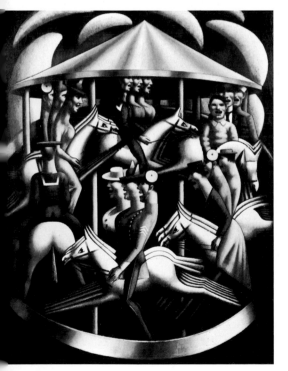

187 The element of genre painting in Gertler's *Merry-go-Round*, 1916, belongs to English tradition rather than to modern continental art, but the artist's effort to translate the scene into emphatic terms of design indicates the extent to which he was endeavouring to assimilate ideas of formal design with his natural tendency towards realism

188 The naïve suggestion but individual quality of Christopher Wood's painting are seen to advantage in coastal paintings of Brittany and Cornwall, such as this *Mending the Nets, Tréboul* of 1930

and little appreciated effort as one of the principal masters of abstract painting at the present time. There is a slight relation in his early work with that of Wood, their common interest in the paintings of a Cornish 'primitive' at St Ives, Alfred Wallis, being reflected in the rudimentary indications of a marine background in some of Nicholson's still-lifes. The influence of Cubist still-life gave rise to some delightful table-tops in which jugs and other familiar objects are combined with scraps of lettering after the Cubist fashion. Yet on the whole more typical of the artist is the arrangement of formal shapes with no attempt at representation, in which an exquisite sense of line and balanced geometrical proportion is combined with colour harmoniously planned with equal sensitiveness and care (*Ill. 189*).

Artist groups formed in the 'between-wars' period, such as the 'Seven and Five' Society of which Nicholson was a member and 'Unit One' signalize a growing trend towards

189 This example of the abstract art of Ben Nicholson, *Vertical Seconds*, of 1953, shows a beautiful sense of balance, proportion, and a linear quality which, though without representational purpose, recalls an ancient English inheritance

190 As in his landscapes, Ivon Hitchens's flower pieces, such as this *Flowers on a Table* of 1958, evoke the sensation of nature in works with an abstract freedom of treatment

the abstraction for which English art offered no precedent and seemed little in accord with the interest in subject-matter it had so strongly displayed in the past. The 'Seven and Five' Society (originally seven painters and five sculptors), first established in 1920, had no more than a loose coherence and the artists associated with it are various in character. A naïve element appears, as already indicated, in the work of Alfred Wallis (1855–1942), Christopher Wood and the early still-lifes of Ben Nicholson. An individual delicacy of colour and sense of pattern is delightfully to be found in the watercolours of David Jones (1895–1974). Frances Hodgkins (1869–

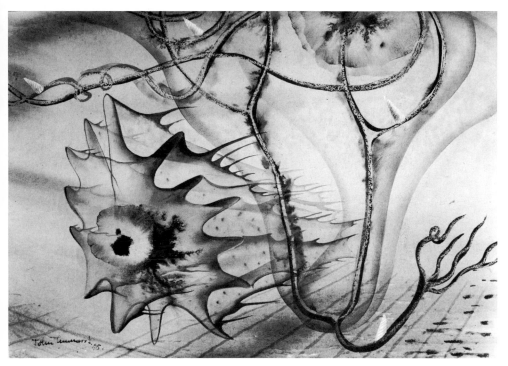

191 After being an early practitioner of abstract art in England, Tunnard developed an imaginative style akin to that of the Surrealists. Without describing natural form this *Sea Flower* of 1955 evokes something of its mystery

1947) developed in middle age a personal mode of giving an abstract unity to landscape and still-life, conceived in low tones and of distinguished effect. Ivon Hitchens (1893–1979) was a pioneer of the kind of painting which retains the feeling or suggestion of nature in a style of abstract freedom and has continued until the present day his distinctive interpretation of the spirit and atmosphere of English country, caught and held in the freedom of brush-stroke (*Ill. 190*).

'Unit One' was an effort early in the 1930s in which Paul Nash had a leading role to give an active unity to English art, though it proved hard to reconcile the aims of the abstract and the imaginative artist. In any case, the abstraction for which English art offered no precedent and which seemed little in accord with the interest in subject-matter it had so strongly displayed in the past was then still a rare and tentative pursuit. The work of John Tunnard (1900–71) is that of an individualist who took to a non-representational form of painting in 1930, though he came to invent a world of his own in which sky, space, and objects with a suggestion of nature appear, having something of Surrealist strangeness (*Ill. 191*). The early 1930s were the period of another kind of abstract painting, the free use of colour in which Geoffrey Tibble (1909–53) and Rodrigo Moynihan (1910–91) showed a marked originality, anticipating the 'Abstract-Expressionism' of the post-war years. Neither painter adhered for long to this boldly experimental course, reverting to figure painting and each producing works of value in this genre. Moynihan who became Professor of Painting at the Royal College of Art in 1948 produced a remarkable *tour de force* of portrait composition in his group of teachers at the College, though in recent years he has again taken up the free abstract painting of which he was one of the pioneers.

Alternative possibilities of revival in imaginative art were suggested by the Surrealist movement, itself a movement of revolt against the purely aesthetic disciplines of the post-Cézanne era and it was welcome to many English artists. It is hardly too much to say that a new era opened as Surrealist influence became transmitted to England in the 1930s to be dramatically proclaimed in the International Surrealist Exhibition in London in 1936. A considerable time before that date, Paul Nash entered on a new phase in which many Surrealist characteristics are to be found – a sense of the strangeness of natural form, of mystery and poetry in land-scape. His naturally poetic temperament was no longer repressed by formal disciplines. The English landscape, always inspiring to him, became in his paintings a land at once familiar and unfamiliar, druidic stones, fabulous earthworks,

192 Sutherland's transition from his early graphic work into an imaginative 'paraphrase' of landscape is marked by the paintings resulting from a visit to Pembrokeshire in 1936, among them being this celebrated *Entrance to a Lane*. Foreground foliage, gleams of light, and distance are united in a vivid mental impression and not as a direct transcript of nature. Though the range of colour is limited the effect is greatly distinguished

the fantasy of fungus shapes giving to his downs and woods an emblematic animation.

It may perhaps be accounted a national trait that the English painters of this phase are distinct from the Surrealists of the Continent in seeking the sanction of nature even for what was dream-like and irrational. The 'found object' which a Marcel Duchamp would display with an ironic humour in the form of a lavatory basin (signed farcically with an invented name) was more seriously considered by Nash. His found objects were the curious manifestations of plant and tree life, his dream world so far had actual existence that he could make records of its components with the aid of a camera. In a similar fashion other artists who have attained present-day eminence sought the marvellous in the real. Henry Moore (1898–1986) could find a world of plastic invention in a worn stone. Graham Sutherland (1903–80) does not so much depart from the Romantic intensity with which Samuel Palmer viewed the lichen on the roof of a barn as carry further this investigation, grafting as he has said a 'new vision on reality' and basing his forms on 'the principles of organic growth'. Yet this, as many remarkable paintings have since shown, was not simply an objective study but a creative process in which a thorn-bush or the gorse on a sea wall take on implications of metaphor, the more impressive because of the exceptional sense of colour and design in which they were embodied (*Ill. 192*).

As painters of Romantic character Graham Sutherland and Francis Bacon (1910–92) may be grouped together. Since 1945 Sutherland's work has shown a surprising variety though the sense of strangeness remains a constant factor, appearing in his studies of a bat or a toad, or in his half-natural, half-mechanical constructions with an eerie fascinating life of their own. Francis Bacon, a self-taught painter who began to exhibit his work in the 1930s, has given an impressive modern variant on the moment of terror which Fuseli conceived, the distortion which Goya saw in human expression, the horror which lurks in modern life. It is part of the effect that he has

193 The close-up of the screaming nurse in the Odessa Steps sequence of Eisenstein's film *The Battleship Potemkin* is the acknowledged source of some of Francis Bacon's most strangely impressive conceptions, that is to say they derive from reality and are not merely the products of a macabre fancy. This relation accounts for a hold upon the spectator which the invented nightmares of Surrealism often fail to make, just as in the late works of Goya it is the credibility of his grimacing figures that makes them disturbingly weird

made that he has shown how often reality is unlike the conventional idea of it – as indeed photography has indicated. It is an aspect of Bacon's originality that he has made creative use of the photograph which so many artists have regarded as a rival or an enemy of painting. The scream of the nurse in Eisenstein's film *The Battleship Potemkin (Ill. 193)* was the origin of that agony with which he convulses the features of a figure adapted from Velazquez's *Pope Innocent X (Ill. 194)*. The photographs in which the pioneer Eadweard Muybridge first stated the truth of human and animal motion have been converted into those lumpish figures which fearfully suggest animality. They may repel as an intimation of a pathological world and yet their creative suggestion for modern painting is not that of Grand Guignol or morbidity but of a fresh look at external reality which does not merely refer back to the conventions of the past but in his words 'deepens the game to be any good at all'.

For a number of painters the Surrealist movement resolved the problem set by a growing interest in abstract art and a hesitation to accept all its implications. It was a stimulating discovery for some that it was possible to make use of both dominating tendencies in modern painting. The paintings of John Tunnard give an instance, and another may be found in the work of Ceri Richards (1903–71) *(Ill. 195)*, an artist of poetic imagination, drawn at one stage towards abstract art but finding a liberation of fancy which Surrealism suggested. It appears in the constructions of painted wood, reliefs of a curious and diverting ingenuity, which he began to produce in 1933. He has since used abstract methods to imaginative ends with notable effect, as in the exhilarating sense of holiday mood and fountain play of the *Trafalgar Square* of 1951 or the sense of depth and translucence in his several variations on the theme of Debussy's *La Cathédrale Engloutie*.

The Surrealist atmosphere of the 1930s stimulated English painters in various ways. Merlyn Evans (1910–73) predisposed to abstract painting as represented by Kandinsky but a contributor to the International Surrealist Exhibition on 1936, has

194 Bacon's adaptations of Velazquez's portrait of *Pope Innocent X* are a unique contribution to modern English painting. The static dignity of the seated figure in the original offers the greatest contrast possible with the sequence of agitated and disturbing expressions the modern painter has given to the face and this perhaps explains his choice of the work as a vehicle

195 The highly individual art of Ceri Richards owes something to Surrealism as a stimulus to the imagination, though a personal response to music and poetry is the vital element. It is recorded that in *The Cycle of Nature* of 1955–6 he based the colour scheme on the suggestions afforded by the garish designs of seed-packets, though the result conveys a deep impression of Dylan Thomas's 'the force that through the green fuse drives the flower'

reserved an intellectual freedom which enables him to use abstract means either in isolation or, for example, for a vigorous evocation of the crowds and bustle of Waterloo Station. The Surrealist atmosphere can be discerned in the minutely detailed imaginary landscapes which Tristram Hillier (1905–83) began to paint early in the 1930s in a style which he later applied to pictures of real places (*Ill. 196*). It tinged with mystery the symbolic figures of Cecil Collins (1908–89) and heightened the imaginative mood in which Edward Burra (1905–76) made his watercolours of sinister and satirical figures, a mood still to be found in the religious compositions to which he later turned. The menacing alignment of forces which the Spanish Civil War brought into the open intensified his change from social caricature in the late 1920s after the manner of George Grosz to paintings of tragic portent. The ominous element of prophecy or warning in Surrealism seemed to find its fulfilment in the 1939–45 war and made it as applicable to its fantastic effects and wreckage as the Cubist-Futurist approach had been to the bleak wastes of the Western Front in 1916 and 1917. The bombed streets depicted by Graham Sutherland, the weird dormitories of the Underground drawn by Henry

196 The sharp outline and detail which distinguish some products of Surrealist painting have been used by Hillier not only to create imaginary scenes but to intensify the impression given by an existing landscape, as in *Fishing Craft at Peniche* of 1959

197, 198 The coloured drawings of shelter scenes in wartime formed a remarkable pictorial addition to Henry Moore's work as a sculptor; these two examples impressively indicate the way in which the subjects stirred the artist's imagination. The drawing (*left*) conveys the fantastic aspect of crowded underground perspectives. In the masterly detailed study of sleepers (*below*), the sculptor's concern with form and structure comes to the fore. In drawings of this kind the artist used combinations of chalk, crayon, watercolour, and pen technique in highly original fashion

199 *Somerset Place, Bath*, one of John Piper's watercolours of 1942, produced by this versatile painter as an official war artist. To an always strong interest in architecture, there was now added an acute awareness of the ravages of bombing, expressed in the vehement contrasts with which he dramatically conveyed the ruin of fine buildings. The sense of drama thus fostered was to animate much of his later work, both in painting and design for the theatre

Moore (*Ills. 197, 198*), the sky-writing of swooping planes in battle painted by Paul Nash have their vivid evidence to give.

As we come nearer to the present there is still that interplay of influence from abroad and independence of an insular kind which as at earlier times makes English painting distinct. It is to be seen in the versatility of John Piper (1903–92), a painter of wide interests who showed himself capable in the 1930s of works of a purely abstract kind but late in that decade reverts to a romantic view of English architecture (*Ill. 199*) and landscape. A reaction against theory and experiment, the conviction that everyday life and local subject still had much to offer the painter is to be seen in the Euston Road School. Started in

200 The deliberate return to painting scenes of everyday life and the avoidance of mannerisms of a modern kind in style are aspects of the Euston Road Group's aims, illustrated by Graham Bell's *The Café* of *c.* 1937–8 which gains distinction from the simplicity and sincerity of the artist's approach. One of those who originated the painting school of 1937–9, he was killed in 1943 while serving as air navigator in the RAF

1937 as a painting school, this association of teachers and pupils working together ceased to be an educational establishment in 1939 with the outbreak of war but the title remained, indicative of an objective approach expressed through a cultivated reticence of style which has not lost its value. Graham Bell (1907–43) gives an example of modern genre, purified of humour and anecdote, in his *The Café*, *c.* 1937–8 (*Ill. 200*). Sir William Coldstream (1908–87) has shown a fastidious quality of style in figure (*Ill. 201*) and portrait painting. Claude Rogers (1907–79) (*Ill. 202*) and Lawrence Gowing (1918–91) (*Ill. 203*) have painted with an admirably

244

201 An unprejudiced and objective attitude to subjects that had always occupied the attention of painters in the past is to be seen in the work of Sir William Coldstream. Studies of the figure carried out with an individual sense of style, as in this *Nude* of 1937, have an important place in his work

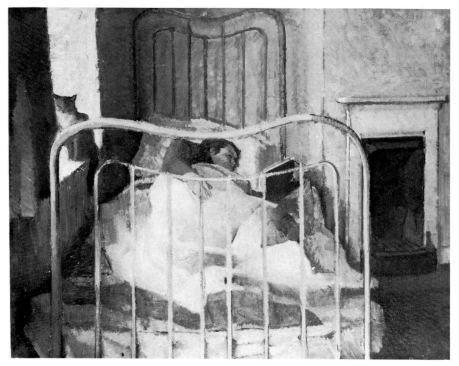

202 *Cottage Bedroom*, 1944, by Claude Rogers, one of the founders of the Euston Road School of painting, 1937–9. In his work there is a combination of essentially painterly qualities of colour and design with the objective view characteristic of this phase of modern English art

unforced and unaffected naturalism. Victor Pasmore (b. 1908) is notable in this group both for the beautiful paintings in which until late in the 1940s he pursued naturalistic ends and his later radical changes of direction to a completely non-pictorial and abstract form of art. In the former category *The Wave*, 1939–44 (*Ill. 204*) is exquisite in atmospheric colour and simplicity of design. His three-dimensional constructions and abstract paintings since about 1950 suggest an evolution outside painting towards a relation of design and architecture (*Ill. 205*).

A number of figure painters came into prominence after the

203 Cultivated reserve, simplicity of conception, and seriousness of manner distinguish this painting of *Judith at sixteen*, 1945, by Gowing who came as a student within the Euston Road sphere of influence

ending of war – John Minton, John Craxton, Robert Colquhoun, and Keith Vaughan. John Minton (1917–57) (*Ill. 206*), a gifted artist whose abilities were adapted alike to figure painting, portraiture, and landscape, had something of the traditional interest in subject-matter closely observed and a flair for graphic illustration, though showing modern influences in some points of style. The tendency of his work might be described as towards a romantic naturalism which he seems to have found hard to reconcile with the drift of the time away from nature. The description 'romantic naturalism' would to some extent apply also to the paintings of John Craxton

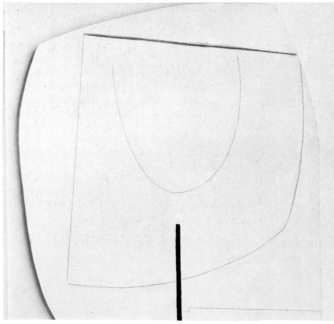

204, 205 While the Euston Road Group, generally speaking, has represented a conservative adherence to picture painting, the remarkable evolution of one of its leaders, Victor Pasmore, indicates the powerful influence of abstract ideas in this century. The two works here reproduced contrast his style of painting in the 1930s with its feeling for atmosphere and natural effect, as in *The Wave* (*above*), and his pursuit in the 1950s and onwards of a purist art tending away from painting towards constructional design, as in *Linear Motif in black and white* of 1960 (*left*)

(b. 1922) as in his studies of pastoral figures and landscape in Greece. Robert Colquhoun (1914–62) shows another aspect of the concern with human subjects which distinguished a whole group in the 1940s (*Ill. 207*). In style deriving something from the sharply cut forms of Wyndham Lewis, but perhaps more from the strongly stylized figure paintings of the Polish artist Jankel Adler (1895–1949) who came to England in 1940, Colquhoun devoted himself to pictures of people, his work taking on an individual character in its depiction of rural and Celtic types of austere dignity, seeming to belong to some

206 *Street Scene in Kingston, Jamaica*, a watercolour by John Minton, whose figure painting in the 1940s displays a feeling for graphic qualities and an observant interest in subject which basically belonged to earlier English tradition

207 Painted in 1946, *Seated Woman with a Cat* is one of a series of pictures in which Colquhoun seems to borrow a formula of design ultimately traceable to the School of Paris but gaining an original force in his application of it to the study of single figures

unchanging mode of primitive life though viewed with modern eyes. Keith Vaughan (1912–77), early acquainted with Suther- land, Minton, and Colquhoun, his paintings and drawings of the 1940s revealing traces of what he derived from each, came

208 From a starting-point related to that of his contemporaries, John Minton and Robert Colquhoun, Keith Vaughan has diverged into paintings of the figure, as in this *Group of Bathers* of 1962, exceptional in English painting in their timeless and generalized aspect and notable for their dramatic power and rich mosaic of colour

into his own in the 1950s and has since developed the classic theme of the nude figure in landscape (in 'assemblies' somewhat recalling the *Bathers* of Cézanne) with powerful result (*Ill. 208*). His later work has derived a fresh stimulus from the brilliant example of the last great luminary of the School of Paris, Nicolas de Staël (1914–55), in the combination of the figure with the abstract suggestion of a rich mosaic of colour. Another style of figure painting is that severe delineation of form and figure which Lucian Freud (b. 1922) has made his own.

The 1950s, however, were years marked by a quite different trend, the movement towards non-representational painting in a free style which the 'Objective-Abstraction' exhibitions in London of the early 1930s had to some extent anticipated. The trend was now reinforced not only by European example but by the 'Abstract-Expressionism' of painters in the United States, which in force and daring made a strong impression on the European continent and England alike. English painting in its abstract aspect was now parallel in course with an international trend of art. Its national character inevitably became less distinct with the submergence or disappearance of subject, though some abstract painters retained the feeling or suggestion of landscape which was so particularly an English tradition. The St Ives painter, Peter Lanyon (1918–64) conveys something of sea and shore as a rarefied suggestion in free abstract works. Robert Medley (b. 1905), William Townsend (1909–73), Alan Reynolds (b. 1926), and Donald Hamilton Fraser (b. 1928) are notable among a number of other artists, evoking rather than representing landscape.

But English abstract painting is various in inspiration and evolution. In the work of William Scott (1913–89) (*Ill. 209*) it has developed from a simplification of the table-top and still-life motif, at one stage showing that equivalence of abstract form and object which de Staël had illuminated and then with a final austerity reducing circular vessels and saucepans to diagrams on a surface. One might find in the variegated bark of the plane tree a likeness to the colours held together in a dark framework in the paintings of William Gear (b. 1915) though this Scottish artist has profited by study of European and American contemporaries and was early in appreciation

209 The development of a completely non-figurative art from the practice of painting a few ordinary components of still-life in as direct and simple a fashion as possible is strikingly represented in *Morning in Mykonos* of 1960–1 by William Scott. The relationship of a few simple shapes is austere but intense in effect, replacing the accidental combinations of still-life objects by an intended division of the canvas as a whole

210 Consciously or otherwise, a number of painters reflect in non-figurative works something of the abstract inquiry of modern science in its explorations of both space and matter. The conception of non-terrestrial space is imaginatively conveyed in the central panel of Denis Bowen's *Triptych for a Venusian* of 1963

of the action painting of Jackson Pollock (with whom he exhibited in New York in 1949).

Other painters evolve abstractions from the figure or aim at an equation of the two; in this respect the works of Peter Kinley (b. 1926) and of Louis Le Brocquy (b. 1916) are notable. Or again, the scientific exploration of space has proposed to the painter some imaginative equivalent as in the dramatically

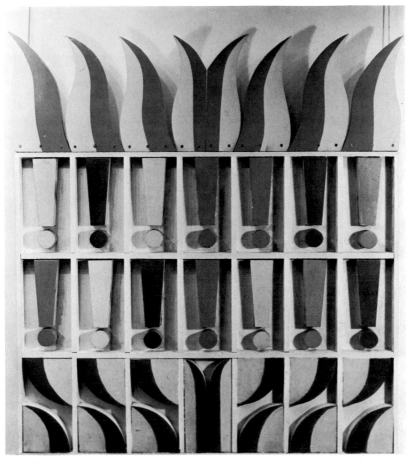

211 The practice of abstract painting and collage has led to various combinations of material and colour which are at once objects and extensions of painting. Striking examples are afforded by the painted wood reliefs of Joe Tilson as in this *Flame Box* of 1963, heraldically brilliant in colour and formal design

conceived works of Denis Bowen (b. 1921) (*Ill. 210*). It is, however a main feature of 'Abstract-Expressionism' to give vent to the force which may be supposed to spring from the subconscious (in this respect it is an end product of the 'automatism' advocated by the Surrealists). The painting of Alan Davie (b. 1920), akin to the American action painting, adds to much vividness of colour what are perhaps to be regarded as vestiges

212 Abstract expression as the product of unpremeditated action, not consciously controlled and in that respect with some points of likeness to American action painting, is exemplified in Davie's *Sacrifice* of 1956. It adds to an exceptional vividness of colour a form of rudimentary symbolism

of a primitive symbolism remaining in the depths of memory (*Ill. 212*). The sheer vigour of colour in itself is exuberantly explored by Avray Wilson (b. 1914). Patrick Heron (b. 1920), Roger Hilton (1911–75), Bryan Wynter (1915–75), and Terry Frost (b. 1915) are artists who have worked with effect in this exploratory field.

The painters of a younger generation, however, seem in the main to have sought for a more definite and geometrical basis

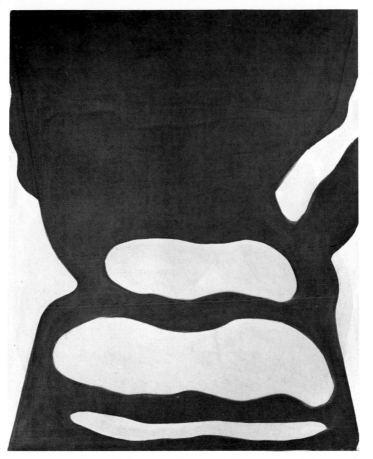

213, 214 Another form of abstract painting which has occupied a number of younger English artists is that of clear-cut outlines and shapes which are to be regarded as of visual interest in themselves and without the psychological associations of 'Abstract-Expressionism'. *12–10–62*, by John Hoyland (*above*) and *Vista City* by Derek Boshier (*below*)

in abstract art, for considered effects of linear pattern, rather than the zest of freely used paint, often with a tendency to substitute other materials for pigment. Examples are given by the symmetrical panels of Robyn Denny (b. 1930), the systems of finely spaced lines of John Hoyland (b. 1934) (*Ill. 213*), the coloured tapes on board of John Plumb (b. 1927), the simplified architectural forms of Derek Hirst (b. 1930). The uncertain element often hard to assess in the informal abstraction, is here replaced by clear geometric definition of a kind which has a recognizable beauty, completely detached from reference to

215 *Blue Beginning*, 1962, an example of paper collage in which Irwin shows resource in many delicate variations of form and subtle tones of colour

216 In contrast with the abstract trend of twentieth-century painting is that of John Bratby, a form of realism, emphatic in statement, in which the artist accepts any aspect of his immediate surroundings as material that may be converted into a picture. *Coach House Door* of 1959 is an example in which the emphasis with which accidental elements are welded into forceful design is of note

nature. Distinctive achievements in design as distinct from picture are to be found in the exquisite paper, wood, and string collages of Gwyther Irwin (b. 1931) (*Ill. 215*) and the painted wood reliefs and structures of Joe Tilson (b. 1928) (*Ill. 211*) who

217 The idea of abstract painting as something other than the rendering of static form, that is, either as an interpretation of light or of movement made optically perceptible, has been variously represented in the art of Jack Smith. Departing from an early realism, as in *Sea Movement* of 1962, for instance, he shows a development somewhat analogous to that of Victor Pasmore

has devised a unique and brilliant kind of modern heraldry which might well serve as an example to the makers of signs and decorative features associated with practical purpose.

In all its forms abstract art is a departure from the picture considered as a window on the world, though it would be strange indeed if the individualism of England had produced no notable reaction in this direction. Criticism in the 1950s hailed the appearance of a new realistic school (sometimes, rather quizzically, termed the 'kitchen-sink school') and for a while, John Bratby (b. 1928) (*Ill. 216*), Jack Smith (b. 1928) (*Ill. 217*), and Edward Middleditch (b. 1923) could be grouped together as painters looking with fresh interest at their immediate surroundings, though their respective aims quickly parted company. It is the study of light, rather than the object on which light falls, that characterizes the later work of Jack Smith. John Bratby, alone, has remained consistent in an objective view of the domestic scene, painting, with an impressive emphasis which is as much Expressionist as realistic, wife and child, breakfast-table, garden, green-house, and the street as viewed through the window-pane. There are other painters who have achieved an individual realism without concession to the twentieth-century concern with manner rather than content. There is some-thing of Hogarthian sturdiness in the work of Ruskin Spear (1911–90), assured in technique, arresting in portraiture (*Ill. 218*), and richly descriptive of the character of popular life in London or by the seaside. Laurence S. Lowry (1887–1976) stands alone as a 'provincial Brueghel' in his depiction of scurrying crowds against backgrounds of factories, chimneys, dingy canals, and the little terrace houses of the industrial town (*Ill. 219*). Carel Weight (b. 1908) adds an imaginative strangeness to the humdrum incident of an average London street or the quietude of a country lane and has shown himself able to picture religious themes, without incongruity, in a realistic modern setting (*Ill. 220*). The work of Derek Hill (b. 1916) gives an instance of a traditional approach to landscape and figure painting, none the less vigorous for being without idiosyncracy of manner.

For painters of a younger generation, however, the widening gap between abstract and representational painting could not be easily bridged, though the effort to make a social comment of some kind or to bring contemporary life again within the artist's range of vision has produced the phenomenon of 'pop art', a label not in itself very satisfactory but roughly indicating an interest in popular imagery. This is not quite the

218 The art of the picture painter concerned with material reality finds an able exponent in Ruskin Spear, in whom one can find affinities with both Hogarth and Sickert in his appreciation of popular life. This *Interior with Nude* continues the Sickert tradition with an entirely painterly quality into which theory does not enter

219 Local attachment in art is not a negligible factor whether it appears in fifteenth-century Florence, or in the Black Country of England in the twentieth century. The art of Lowry, as in this *River Scene* of 1942, gives as impressive a vista of urban industrialism as the local attachment of Renaissance artists gives of more beautiful cities

same thing as painting pictures of popular life though perhaps to be regarded as a step in that direction. Some artists have found curious interest in the fetishes and symbols of modern society. The attitude is suggested by the use Peter Blake (b. 1931) has made of souvenir badges, medals, photographs of film stars, etc., and his ably painted *Self-Portrait with Badges* of 1961 (*Ill. 221*) might be regarded from this point of view as a pictorial manifesto. 'Commercial art', in the form of posters and magazine illustration, has suggested various witty adaptations such as gaily feature in the paintings of Peter Phillips

263

220 The objective view of reality in which, however, there is an imaginative, transforming element going beyond topography, is to be seen in the London paintings of Carel Weight, as in *Albert Bridge*, a view of the embankment and Victorian river bridge

(b. 1939) or ironically in those of Derek Boshier (b. 1939) (*Ill. 214*). Buses and parachute descent are motifs which Allen Jones (b. 1937) has combined with brilliant abstract colour (*Ill. 222*). David Hockney (b. 1937) has gone further than most towards a social theme though if one were to think (without invidious comparison) of his set of *Rake's Progress* etchings in relation to Hogarth's great series, the difference would appear between the amusing or amused modern attitude and

221 In various ways Peter Blake's *Self-Portrait with Badges* of 1961 declares the artist's standpoint – his interest in contemporary life and popular imagery, as represented by the booklet he holds and the collection of contemporary emblems which he wears like medals. It indicates an attitude which has had further expression in the tendencies to which the title 'pop art' has been attached

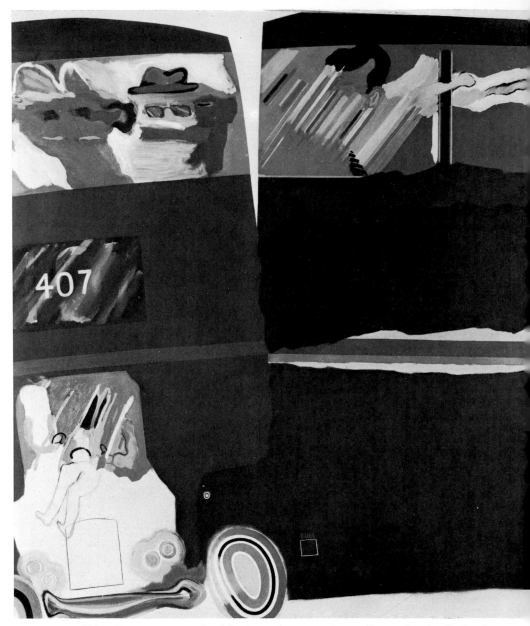

222 Urban imagery not rendered in the static terms of an earlier age but in allusive form is apparent in this *10th Bus Cornering* of 1962 by Allen Jones, one of the younger artists of today. Yet the sense of contemporary life may be thought as vivid in its own way as that of more detailed and descriptive modes of painting

stylization and the effort to create a living world. The productions of the American-born artist, R. B. Kitaj (b. 1932) now settled in England, might be described as a form of allusive comment, sometimes cryptically providing a whole series of 'reflections' in one picture in which thought – of a book or an episode – wanders from one point to another. At the time of writing it would be impossible to say what shape these tendencies (in the work of painters still, mostly, in their twenties) will eventually take; though in general they would seem to be directed to some closer connection with life than abstract art affords.

It must be added to the account of modern English painting, largely centred in London, that there have been separate developments in the British Isles of what might be called a locally nationalist character. In Ireland, Jack Butler Yeats (1871–1957), always a recorder of Irish life and character in drawings and watercolours, produced in later years those passionately coloured oil paintings which seem to express a poetic feeling belonging to both his family and his country and have made him the representative, *par excellence*, of Ireland in visual art. In Scotland also there has been a separate development from that of England, its tradition dating back to the late 1880s and the inspiration then given to the Glasgow 'School' by the works of Corot, Monticelli and Whistler. The tendency since to form artistic alliance with Paris rather than London and also to cultivate an especial force of colour is exemplified in the career and work of J. D. Fergusson (1874–1961) and William MacTaggart (1903–80), the doyens of a vigorous group at the present day. It is tempting to include in the periphery of English painting the remarkable products of Australian artists, all the more as such outstanding painters as Sidney Nolan (1917–92) and Arthur Boyd (b. 1920) have become as much at home in London as in Melbourne; yet Australian painting in style and theme is a subject apart, presenting an exceptional phenomenon in the modern world, the rise of a national school.

Do those qualities which have been singled out as characteristically English in the masters of the past still survive in this century? 'Other times, other manners', it may be said; expression in art changes, if national character does not. Internationalism opposes itself to insularity. In English painting since the last war many threads are intricately entwined though, speaking in general terms, there would seem to be a confident mood, a freedom and vitality of expression which may be looked on as a brilliant fruition of the earlier struggles and enthusiasms of the twentieth century. Yet in addition one may still find something of the long-established feeling for landscape, the old romantic waywardness, the sense of line, the eccentric force which from time to time has given a sudden and extraordinary impulsion to English art; linking, despite many transformations, the present with the past.

Bibliography

Documents

VERTUE, George: *The Notebooks*. Walpole Society, 3 Parts, 1929–34.
Valuable material collected by this early eighteenth-century engraver and antiquary for the history of art in England.

WALPOLE, Horace: *Anecdotes of Painting in England*. First published from Strawberry Hill in 5 vols., 1762–71. Various editions.
Based on Vertue's manuscript but with critical and other addenda.

HILLIARD, Nicholas: *The Art of Limning*. Edited by P. Norman. Walpole Society, 1912.
The Elizabethan miniaturist's own account of technique and view of art.

HOGARTH, William: *The Analysis of Beauty*. 1753.
Exposition of what may be called the rococo aesthetic.

REYNOLDS, Sir Joshua: *The Discourses*. First published 1792. Various editions.
A key work illuminating the artist's view of the European masters, and his English contemporaries.

BLAKE, William: *A Descriptive Catalogue, etc.* 1810.
Account of ideas and methods, contained together with critical comments on art, in the Collected Edition of Blake's Poetry and Prose, Nonesuch Press, 1943.

The Farington Diary. Edited by J. Greig, 8 vols., 1922.
First-hand accounts of artists in the late eighteenth-early nineteenth-century period.

HAYDON, Benjamin Robert: *Autobiography and Journals*. 1847. Various editions.
Classic revelation of ambition and despair.

RUSKIN, Rossetti: *Pre-Raphaelitism*. 1899.
Letters and papers, 1854–62, edited by W. M. Rossetti.

WHISTLER, James McNeill: *The Gentle Art of Making Enemies*. 1890.
Letters and papers including the account of the Ruskin-Whistler case and the aesthetic *credo* of the 'Ten o'Clock' lecture.

BLAST: *Review of the Great English Vortex*. (1) 1914; (2) 1915.
Edited by Wyndham Lewis, the manifesto of Vorticism.

ROTHENSTEIN, Sir William: *Men and Memories*. 2 vols., 1931–2.
Recollections of the art world (1) 1872–1900; (2) 1900–22.

The Oxford History of English Art. Chronological accounts of all branches of visual art as seen against the background of history and fully illustrated (XL vols.). Published volumes are: *English Art: 871–1100* by D. Talbot Rice, 1952. 1100–1216 by T. S. R. Boase, 1953. 1216–1307 by Pieter Brieger, 1957. 1307–1461 by Joan Evans, 1949. 1553–1625 by Eric Mercer, 1962. 1625–1714 by Margaret Whinney and Oliver Millar, 1957. 1800–1870 by T. S. R. Boase, 1959.

BINYON, Laurence: *The Followers of William Blake.* 1925.
  Important for the study of Samuel Palmer and his friends.
CHESNEAU, Ernest: *The English School of Painting.* English translation with an Introduction by Ruskin, 1885.
  A French view of English painting in the nineteenth century.
CROFT-MURRAY, Edward: *Decorative Painting in England.* 1963.
  Painting as the complement to architecture from Tudor times to Sir James Thornhill.
DICKES, W. F.: *The Norwich School of Painting.* 1905.
FRY, Roger: *Reflections on British Painting.* 1934.
  A critical study from the anti-literary standpoint.
GAUNT, William: *The Pre-Raphaelite Tragedy.* 1942.
GRANT, Col.: *Chronological History of the Old English Landscape Painters.* 2 vols. n.d.
  Including accounts of many minor masters.
HUGHES, C. E.: *Early English Water Colour.* First published 1913. Revised and edited by Jonathan Mayne, 1960.
HUNT, W. Holman: *Pre-Raphaelitism and the Pre-Raphaelite Brotherhood.* 1905.
  A main if in some respects biased source of information.
LAMB, Sir Walter: *The Royal Academy.* 1935.
PEVSNER, Nikolaus: *The Englishness of English Art.* 1951. Reith Lectures, 1955–6.
  A stimulating inquiry into the continuance of tradition.
READ, Sir Herbert: *Contemporary British Art.* 1951.
REDGRAVE, R. and S.: *A Century of Painters of the English School.* First published 1866. Revised edition, 1947.
ROTHENSTEIN, Sir John: *Modern English Painters.* 2 vols., 1952–6. (1) Sickert to Smith; (2) Lewis to Moore.
  The Tate Gallery. 1962.
SITWELL, Sacheverell: *Conversation Pieces.* 1936.
TAYLOR, Basil: *Animal Painting in England.* 1955.
WATERHOUSE, Ellis: *Painting in Britain, 1530–1790.* 1953.
  Admirable application of modern scholarship to a comprehensive study.
WHITLEY, W. T.: *Artists and their Friends in England.* 2 vols. (1) 1700–1799; (2) 1800–1820.
WILENSKI, R. H.: *English Painting.* 1933.
WILLIAMS, Iolo: *Early English Water Colours.* 1952.
  The most comprehensive work on the subject.

Individual Artists

CUNNINGHAM, Allan: *The Lives of the Most Eminent English Painters*. First published 1829–33. Continued by Mrs Charles Heaton to include Victorian painters. 3 vols., 1879–80.
> Anecdotal biographies of the masters.

BLUNT, Sir Anthony: *The Art of William Blake*. 1959.

GILCHRIST, Alexander: *Life of William Blake*. First published 1863. Edition edited by Ruthven Todd, Everyman Library, 1942.

WILSON, Mona: *Life of William Blake*. 1927.

SHIRLEY, Hon. Andrew: *Bonington*. 1940.

LESLIE, C. R.: *Memoirs of the Life of John Constable*. First published 1843; illustrated edition with notes by Hon. Andrew Shirley, 1937.

OPPÉ, A. P.: *Alexander and Robert Cozens*. 1952.

BAKER, C. H. Collins: *Crome*. 1921.

FARR, Dennis: *William Etty*. 1958.
> With catalogue and illustrations.

FRITH, W. P.: *My Autobiography and Reminiscences*. 3 vols., 1887–8.

WATERHOUSE, Ellis K.: *Gainsborough*. 1958.
> Complete catalogue, illustrated, with Introduction.

WHITLEY, W. T.: *Thomas Gainsborough*. 1915.
> The standard life.

GIRTIN, T. and LOSHAK, D.: *The Art of Thomas Girtin*. 1954.

AUERBACH, E.: *Nicholas Hilliard*. 1961.

ANTAL, Frederick: *Hogarth and his Place in European Art*. 1962.
> His relationship with Continental art traced with great learning.

BECKETT, R. B.: *Hogarth*. 1949.
> The best illustrated modern account of the man and his work.

NICHOLS, J.: *Biographical Anecdotes of W. Hogarth*. 1781.

JOHN, Augustus: *Chiaroscuro*. Autobiography. 1952.

ROTHENSTEIN, Sir John: *Augustus John*. 1944.

GARLICK, Kenneth: *Sir Thomas Lawrence*. 1954.
> With catalogue and illustrations.

BAKER, C. H. Collins: *Lely and the Stuart Portrait Painters*. 1912.

BECKETT, R. B.: *Lely*. 1951.

MILLAIS, J. G.: *The Life of Sir John Millais*. 2 vols., 1899.

READ, Sir Herbert: *Henry Moore: Sculpture and Drawings*. 1949.

BERTRAM, A.: *Paul Nash, Portrait of an Artist*. 1955.

READ, Sir Herbert: *Ben Nicholson*. 2 vols., 1948–56.

GRIGSON, Geoffrey: *Samuel Palmer. The Visionary Years*. 1947.
> Perceptive biography with catalogue and illustrations.

PALMER, A. H.: *The Life and Letters of Samuel Palmer*. 1892.

SMART, Alastair: *The Life and Art of Allan Ramsay*. 1952.
> A modern reappraisal of a long neglected master.

NORTHCOTE, J.: *Memoirs of Sir Joshua Reynolds, Knt*. 2 vols., 1813–15.

WATERHOUSE, Ellis K.: *Reynolds*. 1941.
> Excellent modern account, illustrated and with catalogue.

DOUGHTY, O.: *Dante Gabriel Rossetti.* 1957.
GREGO, J.: *Rowlandson the Caricaturist.* 1880.
OPPÉ, A. P.: *Thomas Rowlandson.* 1923.
BROWSE, Lillian: *Sickert.* 1943.
  Introduction and fully illustrated catalogue.
EMMONS, Robert: *The Life and Opinions of Walter Richard Sickert.* 1941.
COLLIS, Maurice: *Intimate Biography of Stanley Spencer.* 1962.
ROTHENSTEIN, Elizabeth: *Stanley Spencer.* 1945.
  Book of illustrations with Introduction.
IRONSIDE, Robin: *Wilson Steer.* 1943.
  Book of illustrations with Introduction.
COOPER, Douglas: *Graham Sutherland.* 1961.
  A critical appreciation, fully illustrated and documented.
FINBERG, A. J.: *The Life of J. M. W. Turner, R.A.* 1939. Revised with a supplement, 1961.
  The authoritative modern life with catalogue.
THORNBURY, Walter: *The Life of J. M. W. Turner, R.A.* 1861.
  The first biography (confused and unreliable).
LAVER, James: *Whistler.* 1930. Revised edition 1951.
The Life of James McNeill Whistler. 2 vols., 1908.
  An essential biography for information rather than critical soundness.
CUNNINGHAM, Allen: *The Life of Sir David Wilkie.* 3 vols., 1843.
CONSTABLE, W. G.: *Richard Wilson.* 1953.
  An authoritative modern work.

The Penguin Modern Painters Series (1944) includes the following albums with biographical and critical essays and illustrations in black and white and in colour. Raymond Mortimer: *Duncan Grant.* Robin Ironside: *David Jones.* Geoffrey Grigson: *Henry Moore.* Herbert Read: *Paul Nash.* Philip Hendy: *Matthew Smith.* Clive Bell: *Victor Pasmore.* John Betjeman: *John Piper.* E. Sackville-West: *Graham Sutherland.*

List of Illustrations

Measurements are given in inches. Height precedes width

273

MYTENS, David (*c.* 1590–1642)
Charles I as Prince of Wales, 1623
Oil on canvas, 80¾ × 57
Royal Collection, Windsor
By gracious permission of Her Majesty
    the Queen   21

NASH, Paul (1889–1946)
Northern Adventure, 1929–41
Oil on canvas, 35½ × 28
Art Gallery and Industrial Museum,
    Aberdeen   185

NEVINSON, Christopher Richard
    Wynne, ARA (1889–1946)
Star Shell, *c.* 1916
Oil on canvas, 20 × 16
Courtesy the Trustees of the Tate Gallery,
    London   182

NICHOLSON, Ben (1895–1982)
Vertical Seconds, 1953
Oil on canvas, 29 × 19
Courtesy the Trustees of the Tate Gallery,
    London   189

NICHOLSON, Sir William (1872–1949)
Gurnards, 1931
Oil on canvas, 12 × 16
Private Collection, England   163

OCLE (?) (active 14th century)
Retable (5 panels), 14th century
Norwich Cathedral
Photo copyright 'Country Life'   5

OLIVER, Isaac (d. 1617)
Young Man leaning against a Tree (Sir
    Philip Sidney?), *c.* 1590
Miniature, vellum on cardboard, 5 × 3½
Royal Collection
By gracious permission of Her Majesty
    the Queen   17

OLIVER, Isaac
Portrait of Richard Sackville, Earl of
    Dorset, 1616
Miniature, 9¼ × 6
Courtesy Victoria and Albert Museum,
    London
Crown Copyright   18

OPIE, John, RA (1761–1807)
The Peasant's Family, *c.* 1783–5
Oil on canvas, 59 × 71
Courtesy the Trustees of the Tate Gallery,
    London   75

ORPEN, Sir William, RA (1878–1931)
A Bloomsbury Family, 1907
Oil on canvas, 33½ × 35
Scottish National Gallery of Modern Art
    171

PALMER, Samuel (1805–81)
A Shoreham Garden, *c.* 1829
Watercolour and gouache, 11 × 8¾
Courtesy Victoria and Albert Museum,
    London   113

PARIS, Matthew (d. 1259)
Virgin and Child. From Matthew Paris,
    'Historia Anglorum', before 1259
Drawing, 14 × 9¾
Courtesy the Trustees of the British
    Museum   4

PASMORE, Victor (b. 1908)
The Wave, 1939–44
Oil on canvas, 36 × 28
Collection Sir Kenneth Clark, Hythe,
    Kent   204

PASMORE, Victor
Linear Motif in black and white, 1960
Oil on wood, 48½ × 48½
New London Gallery, London   205

PIPER, John (1903–92)
Somerset Place, Bath, 1942
Watercolour, 18 × 29
Courtesy the Trustees of the Tate Gallery,
    London   199

PISSARRO, Lucien (1863–1944)
Crockers Lane, Coldharbour, 1916
Oil on canvas, 25¾ × 21¼
City Art Galleries, Manchester   173

PRYDE, James (1866–1941)
The Slum, 1916
Private Collection
Photo Arts Council of Great Britain   162

RAEBURN, Sir Henry, RA (1756–1823)
Portrait of Colonel Alastair Macdonell of
    Glengarry (1771–1828)
Oil on canvas, 95 × 59
National Gallery of Scotland, Edinburgh
    80

RAMSAY, Allan (1713–84)
Portrait of Margaret Lindsay, *c.* 1755
Oil on canvas, 29¼ × 24⅜
National Gallery of Scotland, Edinburgh
    51

281

282

TUNNARD, John (1900–71)
Sea Flower, 1955
Gouache, 10¼ × 14½
Collection Mr and Mrs Charles Wrinch,
Guernsey   191

TURNER, Joseph Mallord William, RA
(1775–1851)
Salisbury Cathedral: View from the
Cloister
Watercolour, 26¾ × 19½
Courtesy Victoria and Albert Museum,
London
Crown Copyright   87

TURNER, Joseph Mallord William
Calais Pier. An English Packet arriving,
1802–3
Oil on canvas, 35½ × 47½
Courtesy the Trustees of the Tate Gallery,
London   115

TURNER, Joseph Mallord William
The Passage of the St Gotthard, 1804
Watercolour, 40½ × 27
Collection Mr Esmond Morse   116

TURNER, Joseph Mallord William
The Thames near Windsor, c. 1807
Oil on thin veneer, 7 × 10¼
Courtesy the Trustees of the Tate Gallery,
London   117

TURNER, Joseph Mallord William
Snowstorm: Hannibal and his Army
crossing the Alps, 1810–12
Oil on canvas, 57 × 93
Courtesy the Trustees of the Tate Gallery,
London   121

TURNER, Joseph Mallord William
Crossing the Brook, 1815
Oil on canvas, 76 × 65
Courtesy the Trustees of the Tate Gallery,
London   120

TURNER, Joseph Mallord William
Ulysses deriding Polyphemus, c. 1829
Oil on canvas, 52¼ × 80
Courtesy the Trustees of the National
Gallery, London   122

TURNER, Joseph Mallord William
Fire at Sea, c. 1834
Oil on canvas, 68½ × 88
Courtesy the Trustees of the Tate Gallery,
London   119

TURNER, Joseph Mallord William
Interior at Petworth (unfinished), 1837
Oil on canvas, 35¾ × 47¼
Courtesy the Trustees of the Tate Gallery,
London   123

TURNER, Joseph Mallord William
Snowstorm: Steamboat off a harbour
mouth making signals in shallow water
and going by the lead, 1842
Oil on canvas, 35½ × 47½
Courtesy the Trustees of the Tate Gallery,
London   118

VAUGHAN, Keith (1912–77)
Group of Bathers, 1962
Oil on canvas, 24 × 24
Private Collection   208

WALKER, Frederick, ARA (1840–75)
Autumn, 1865
Watercolour, 24¼ × 19⅝
Courtesy Victoria and Albert Museum,
London
Crown Copyright   154

WALKER, Robert (c. 1605/10–56/8)
Portrait of Cromwell
Oil on canvas, 49½ × 39½
National Portrait Gallery, London   25

WALLIS, Henry (1830–1916)
Death of Chatterton, 1856
Oil on canvas, 23¾ × 35¾
Courtesy the Trustees of the Tate Gallery,
London   140

WALTON, Henry (1746–1813)
Girl Buying a Ballad, RA 1778
Oil on canvas, 37 × 29
Collection the Hon. Mrs John Mildmay-
White   69

WARD, James, RA (1769–1859)
Bulls Fighting with view of Donatt's
Castle, Glamorganshire in the distance
Oil on panel, 51¾ × 89½
Courtesy Victoria and Albert Museum,
London   114

WATTS, George Frederick, OM, RA
(1817–1904)
Portrait of Ellen Terry
Oil on canvas, 23½ × 23½
National Portrait Gallery, London   152

Index

Italic figures denote pages on which illustrations appear